TAKING ON TURNOVER

AN ACTION GUIDE FOR CHILD CARE CENTER TEACHERS AND DIRECTORS

I I I

Marcy Whitebook
Dan Bellm

Center for the Child Care Workforce
Washington, D.C.

The Center for the Child Care Workforce (CCW) was founded in 1978 as the Child Care Employee Project, and was known as the National Center for the Early Childhood Work Force from 1994 to 1997. CCW is a nonprofit research, education and advocacy organization committed to improving child care quality by upgrading the compensation, working conditions and training of child care teachers and family child care providers. CCW coordinates two major efforts to promote leadership and career advancement for teachers and providers: the Worthy Wage Campaign and the Early Childhood Mentoring Alliance.

ACKNOWLEDGMENTS

Taking On Turnover™ is based on a series of training programs for child care teachers and directors, developed and implemented for the Center for the Child Care Workforce by Marcy Whitebook, Alice Burton and Jean Monroe, with assistance from Dibsy Machta and Laura Sakai. Jan Brown, Sharon Hawley, Lisa Lee and Carol Sharpe also attended training sessions and provided very helpful feedback.

We would like to thank the teachers and directors of the following 20 San Francisco Bay Area child care programs who participated in our six-month pilot Managing Turnover Project training in 1997: Aquatic Park School, Association of Children's Services, Child Education Center, Davis Street Community Center Preschool Program, Dimock House, Duck's Nest, Ephesians Child Development Center, Family Service Agency Child Development Center, Genentech's Second Generation, Geo Kids, Happy Hall School, Intercommunal Survival School, Merry Moppet Preschool, Palcare, Leo Ryan Child Development Center, St. John's Preschool, Step One Preschool, Skyline College Children's Center, Tri Cities Children's Centers, and Via Nova Children's School. We would also like to thank the many child care program administrators who participated in our *Taking On Turnover*™ training sessions throughout California in 1997 and 1998.

Thanks also to Marci Andrews, Gerri DiLisi, Julie Olsen Edwards, Dan Fishkin, Robert French, Peggy Haack, Jennifer Kagiwada, Jessica Mihaly, Wendy Rakower, Paula Sherman, Rosemarie Vardell and Claudia Wayne, who reviewed early drafts and offered a wealth of helpful comments.

Finally, our special thanks to the David and Lucile Packard Foundation, which has generously supported the various phases of our work on turnover since 1994. Thanks also to the Packard Foundation, the San Francisco Foundation, the Trio Foundation and the California State Department of Education, for supporting our turnover training efforts in California in 1997 and 1998.

Printed in the U.S.A. by Harris Lithographics, Inc.
Book design: Elaine Joe

ISBN 1-889956-14-7

Center for the Child Care Workforce
733 15th Street, N.W., Suite 1037
Washington, D.C. 20005-2112
Tel.: (202) 737-7700 / (800) U-R-WORTHY
Fax: (202) 737-0370
E-mail: ccw@ccw.org
Web site: http://www.ccw.org

TABLE OF CONTENTS

PREFACE

"Mommy, who's going to be my teacher today?," a four-year-old boy asked his mother on the way to child care one morning. There should have been a simple answer: why, his new teacher Nancy, of course. But his anxiety underscored a far-from-simple problem: there had been three changes in caregivers at the program over six months' time, and his nagging sense of doubt was only matched by the knot growing in his mother's stomach.

When the boy asked, "And is Nancy going to stay?," his mother did her best to reassure him that Nancy would be there at least until he left for kindergarten. So his expression lightened, and he proceeded to rattle off a list of things he liked to do with his teacher. But the truth was that his mother didn't know whether Nancy— or any of the teachers, for that matter— could afford to finish out the year, even though she also knew her son couldn't afford for them to leave. He had faced enough change already, and it was diminishing his sense of trust in the world at an age when building trust is all-important. What could she really say or do to ease his mind?

This workbook and action guide, *Taking On Turnover*, is the result of our efforts at the Center for the Child Care Workforce (CCW) over the past decade to understand and address the impact of staff turnover in child care settings. It is designed to help teaching staff and administrators explore together how to make your child care center a place where you and your co-workers can

grow and develop as practitioners, and provide the best possible stability and continuity for children and families.

We were first spurred on to develop policies and programs to build a more skilled and stable child care workforce when our National Child Care Staffing Study, in 1988, clearly documented the relationship between high staff turnover, low-quality services, and negative consequences for children in center-based care. But while the issues of promoting a *skilled* workforce, through training and professional development programs, have generally been easier to address, and have been more readily embraced by funders and policy makers, it has proven far more challenging to *stabilize* this workforce.

Although child care teachers and providers have above-average levels of education and training among U.S. workers, at least one-third of them continue to leave the job each year—a trend which is nearly double the overall U.S. job turnover rate (Bureau of Labor Statistics, 1998). No matter how far our child care training systems evolve, they have clearly solved only a small part of the problem if we cannot *retain* the people we have trained. As one experienced trainer has observed to us, "I feel like I'm constantly filling a bucket of water with a hole in it."

In the child care profession as a whole, our response to turnover has generally been one of silence. Scarce resources often make turnover seem impossible to solve. Above all, it's very hard to offer the kind of wages and benefits that will encourage well-quali-fied people to stay in child care. Ironically, it some-times seems that our deep-ening awareness of the turnover problem has squelched the very dia-logue that is required to address it—whether it's due to the numbing effect of dealing with constant changes in staffing, embar-rassment about a phenomenon that's associated with negative outcomes for children, or a belief that only huge amounts of money for salaries will relieve the problem at all. Sometimes, programs intentionally remain silent about turnover to maintain an appear-ance of normalcy for parents and the public, not wishing to raise alarm.

Even worse, we in the child care field have often been socialized to believe that it's unprofessional to talk about money—and in the name of being inclusive, many of us also have a hard time saying 'no' to anyone who isn't right for the job. Both of these add

At least one-third of the child care workforce leaves the job each year—nearly double the overall U.S. job turnover rate.

up to powerful forces that maintain our professional silence and inaction on turnover. But unless we "take on" turnover and break the silence that has surrounded it, the problem can only continue to worsen year after year.

In April 1994, the Center for the Child Care Workforce was able to bring together child care practitioners, advocates, policy makers, funders and researchers for a two-day forum on improving compensation. Among the highlights of that meeting was a pre-sentation by M.-A. Lucas, Chief of Child and Youth Services of the U. S. Army, who shared how her pro-grams had found a way to measure the costs of staff turnover and tackle the problem head-on. Four years before, Military Child Care had instituted a system-wide caregiver compensation and training plan after calculating that the plan would be no more expensive than the costs they were already facing from staff turnover—which was as high as 300 percent a year at some bases.

"It was critical for us to cost out the price of high versus low turnover," Ms. Lucas said. "When we tracked the expense of training and retraining, con-ducting multiple background checks, all the administrative costs borne by the child care facilities and our support services, it was a 'wash.' When we brought these indirect costs out into the open, we saw that they were just about as much as the direct cost of raising salaries." The plan has dramatically reduced turnover, increased salaries, improved training activities, and raised overall program quality—all for roughly the same cost as the old high-turnover system (Bellm, 1994).

While participants in the forum knew that most individual programs and communities would not be able to make such progress so soon, we strongly felt that the child care field should be exploring how to put more resources into turnover management and prevention. That year, we were fortunate to receive funding from the David and Lucile Packard Foundation to explore the concept of "the high cost of turnover" in civilian child care settings, and to investigate how other industries manage and reduce turnover in the workforce. A second grant from the Packard Foundation two years later, augmented by support from the San Francisco Foundation and the Trio Foundation, allowed us to carry out a six-month training and research project, working with 20 directors and 40 teaching staff from San Francisco Bay Area centers to explore strategies to calculate turnover-related costs, cope more effectively with turnover when it occurs, and implement programmatic changes to increase staff stability. Most recently, in 1998, we received support from the California State Department of Education and the Packard Foundation to conduct a shorter version of this training throughout California.

HOW TO USE THIS BOOK: OBJECTIVES AND ASSUMPTIONS

Taking On Turnover closely follows the structure of our California-based training projects, and shares the same three objectives:

1. to break the silence around turnover in the child care profession;

2. to deepen our understanding of turnover by learning from other industries how to manage and reduce it; and

3. to clarify what each of us can do about turnover, both within individual programs and throughout the field.

This workbook is intended for center-based child care teachers, assistant teachers, administrators (whether on- or off-site), trainers, union representatives, and anyone who is involved in recruiting and retaining child care staff. It is applicable to programs serving any age group, and operating under any kind of funding or ownership structure. It can also be used in a variety of meeting and training formats—whether in a series of staff meetings or workshops, at a weekend retreat, or in a multi-week course devoted to the topics of staff turnover and retention.

Although you may start by reading this book by yourself, turnover is not something that you can solve on your own. First and foremost, we believe that you have to talk with your co-workers about it, and *Taking On*

Turnover contains concrete suggestions on how to go about the task. Ideally, this workbook will be useful whether you read it all the way through on your own, consult all or part of it as a resource for a workshop or class, or use it as an action guide to focus on turnover within your center or community. You don't need to do every activity in the book in order to benefit from it. We realize that dealing with turnover may seem like an insurmountable problem, and that everyone in the field has many duties to juggle already. But it's better to start small than not to start at all! Each section contains:

➡ reading material about a particular subject related to managing or reducing turnover; and

➡ exercises, worksheets and/or discussion topics that you can use on your own or in a group.

In the back of the book, on page 159, you will also find an extensive list of references and suggestions for further reading.

If you begin this book thinking that low wages and poor benefits are the *only* causes of turnover, we hope you will end by reflecting on other contributing factors as well. If you are convinced that people leave your workplace only for personal reasons, this book will encourage you to think about compensation, personnel policies, workplace relationships, and issues of cultural diversity, and how these might be contributing to staff members' decisions to stay or go. As you find new or different ways to think about the turnover problem, we hope that this, in turn, will stimulate new ideas on your part about how to actively tackle turnover in your center and community.

> **Unless we break the silence that has surrounded turnover in child care, the problem will only continue to worsen year after year.**

In general, the "you" whom the book addresses includes anyone who works in center-based child care or a related field, and who is affected by child care staff turnover. In some cases, particular discussions or activities more appropriate for directors or teachers, or both together, will be indicated accordingly.

Please note also that we generally use female pronouns when referring to teachers and administrators, since 98 percent of the U.S. child care workforce are women, and because it becomes awkward to repeatedly say "he/she" and "his/her." But we would also like to recognize the importance of men working in the field of early care and education, and hope that both men and women will feel included and spoken to as they read this material.

The book also reflects three major assumptions, based on our experiences with directors and teaching staff during the course of our trainings:

1. Each of us has a wealth of "turnover experience" to draw upon.

In all of our training sessions, we have asked participants to share how long they have been in the child care field, how many child care-related jobs they have held, and how many "turnover events" they have witnessed in the past five years (see page 10). This simple exercise has demonstrated powerfully that all of us in child care are turnover experts—and our vast experience, both positive and negative, can help us build solutions. We know how turnover affects us, our co-workers, and the children and families we serve. We can turn that experience to our advantage by reflecting upon those periods of turnover that have been painful or difficult, and others that have gone more smoothly. In many ways, we already know what works and what doesn't.

2. Collective solutions to workplace problems are the most effective.

This book emphasizes group participation in solving problems on the job. Our decision to make it an action-oriented workbook for teachers *and* directors reflects our strong conviction that both perspectives are indispensable in reducing and managing turnover. Too often in child care settings, the director is looked to as the person who should

> **ASSUMPTIONS**
>
> Each of us is a "turnover expert."
>
> Collective solutions to workplace problems are best.
>
> Taking on turnover requires effort both within our individual programs, and beyond.

fix everything, or she takes this role upon herself. While directors should be leaders who help set an overall tone and climate for the workplace, everyone in the setting has opinions, feelings and ideas about how it can function most smoothly. Teaching staff are often more closely attuned to the daily flow of classrooms, and this might lead them to reach different conclusions from directors about ideal staffing patterns. Directors are often more aware of the budgetary implications of program decisions, which teachers may not take into account when they make proposals. What's most important is to create a climate of real dialogue, so that solutions can emerge that are based on different points of view and areas of knowledge. In multi-site agencies, the central administration should also seek out and use the day-to-day expertise of teaching staff and site directors. Too often, the alternative is "solutions" that fail because too few of the people who are affected have participated in or embraced them.

3. Taking on turnover requires two levels of effort: both within individual child care centers and beyond.

As we have already noted, a serious shortage of resources holds the child care field back in many ways, and

ACTIVITY

WE ARE TURNOVER EXPERTS: AN INFORMAL SURVEY

Try the following exercise on your own, or during a staff meeting or community discussion. If you do it with others, ask everyone to write their calculations for each item on a separate piece of paper. Then add up the totals for each. Be sure to bring a calculator if it is a large group! (In one training session, a group of 35 people estimated that they had gone through more than 92 job changes and witnessed at least 1,300 turnover events.)

➤ **Calculate the following:**

• The number of years you have been in the child care field.

• The number of child care-related jobs you have held. (This will give you a rough idea of how many job changes the group has made.)

• The number of turnover events you have witnessed during the past five years, or during your career. (While this number might depress you, it can also help you recognize how much you know about what causes people to stay or leave, and what makes departures better or worse.)

• The number of skilled teachers you personally know who have left the child care field.

➤ **As you make these calculations, think about:**

• The best and worst job departure you have personally experienced. What helped? Or what made it a bad experience?

• One of the skilled teachers you know who has left child care. Share a story about this person. Why did she leave? What is she doing now? What do you especially miss about her teaching skills? (These are also good questions to ask parents.)

➤ **After you analyze the results, consider sharing them:**

• With parents in your newsletter,

• In a letter to the editor of your local newspaper, or

• In a letter to one of your elected officials, as a way of explaining why we must "take on turnover" in child care.

there are limits to what an individual center can do to stabilize its workforce. The final section of this book discusses the kinds of coordinated effort by practitioners throughout the field that will be necessary in order to strengthen our nation's child care system, and to make child care a profession that many people can choose to stay in throughout a long career. But at the same time, this need for long-term advocacy should not stop us from beginning, *right now*, to "take on turnover" within our own workplaces in whatever ways we can. And if you are part of a multi-site agency, the site-based staff have to be involved in these efforts; it's not really possible to "take on turnover" at arm's length. Until we all begin to discuss and explore turnover more explicitly with each other, we run the risk of overlooking the aspects of the problem that are within our power to fix.

We hope that this book will help you to begin, to take action, and to move ahead.

THE ABC CHILD CARE CENTER: A TURNOVER STORY

(This story was written in 1992 for the Worthy Wage Campaign by the Seattle-based early childhood trainers and advocates Margie Carter and Deb Curtis. Since that time, it has been used in hundreds of training sessions and advocacy meetings around the country. We reprint it here with the authors' permission because it captures so many of the issues involved in "taking on turnover" in child care centers.)

ARTIST/ILLUSTRATOR: JOAN NEWCOMB

Once upon a time—it could have been yesterday or today—ABC Child Care Center served families with children from six weeks to five years old. ABC Child Care is a happy, loving place where people have worked hard to create a family environment. Three years ago, the program became accredited by the National Association for the Education of Young Children.

This is Cathy. She used to work at ABC Child Care, but left three months ago to work as a parking lot attendant for $12.00 an hour. Cathy is still friends with people at ABC. She didn't want to leave. She loved working with children and even took some child development classes to get better at it.

Here is Cathy on the phone to Sonja, a teacher who still works at ABC.

"Sonja, I really miss the kids."

"They really miss you too. Casaundra asks about you every day."

"Oh, don't tell me that. I feel so bad. My new job is really boring. It doesn't challenge me at all. Here, if I make a mistake, the only harm that's done is money lost on a parking stall.

"But I make so much more money that I'm getting all my bills paid off. You know what? They're going to be hiring again. I told my boss I knew someone who might want the job.

"What do you think?"

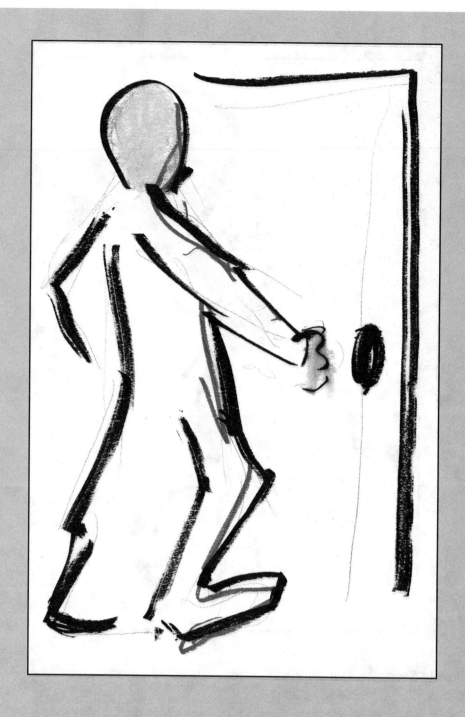

Sonja is torn, but knows she can't resist this offer. She's already had to train two people since Cathy left. Sonja is exhausted, frustrated and having a harder and harder time stretching her pay check to make ends meet. She goes to Joyce, the director, to tell her she's leaving for a better-paying job.

Ted is Sonja's co-teacher. He is an enthusiastic, bright young man who thought it would be fun to work with kids. Ted has no background in child development or experience juggling the multitude of tasks involved in running a classroom.

He's alone in the room right now while Sonja is off talking to the director. It's hard for him when his co-teacher leaves, even for a few minutes. Both he and the children depend on her a great deal.

See Joyce, the director of ABC Child Care, with her head in her hands. See the tears in her eyes. See the scream forming inside her. See all the names crossed off her substitute teacher list.

In the last six months, Joyce has had to find four new teachers. How will she ever be able to reassure the parents in Sonja's room, now that Sonja is leaving?

Here is Maria, who has two children: Malcolm, eight months old, and Casaundra, age four. Maria was glad to find ABC. It seemed just right for her family's needs. But one month after she enrolled her children, one of Malcolm's caregivers left. Then Casaundra's favorite teacher, Cathy, left.

Maria has a lot of stress on her job, and her children have started waking her up several times during the night. But who can she talk to about her concerns for her children? She had just begun to confide in Cathy, and now Cathy is gone.

Casaundra has learned to write her name. Ever day she works at the art table making pictures with hearts. She always asks Ted or Sonja to help her write "TO CATHY" on her hearts. Today she is making a picture for Sonja too.

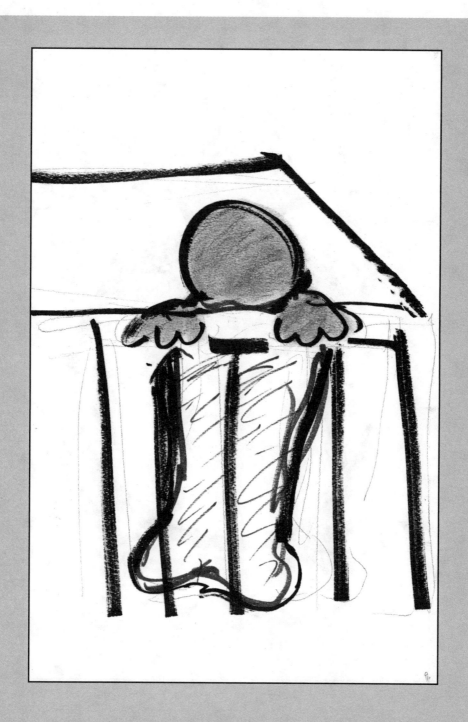

Malcolm is in the infant room. He cries a lot more than he used to. He's driving his new caregiver crazy.

There is no end to this story. It is repeating itself over and over again in child care centers all across our country. This is a story that needs to be told in all kinds of settings, to all kinds of people. It is not a naptime story.

Telling this story must wake people up before it is too late.

ACTIVITIES

USING THE ABC STORY

➠ Read the ABC Story at a staff, parent and/or board meeting to introduce a discussion on how to "take on turnover" at your program. You may also want, as many others have done, to photocopy enlargements of these pages to make an oversized, easy-to-read version of the book. (Children can help decorate or color it, too.)

➠ Try a group role play in which different people adopt the roles of the various characters in the story, to explore the ways that turnover personally affects teachers, administrators, children and parents. Or role play one of the scenes: for example, when Sonja goes in to talk to the director.

➠ Either as a group or on your own, write a sequel to the ABC Story. What happens next? Does the situation get worse? Does it get turned around for the better? For example:

✓ What if Sonja enticed Cathy back to her old job?

✓ What if Maria decided to talk to other parents and take their concerns to the Board?

✓ What if Joyce took these turnover problems to the whole staff and asked for their help?

Part 1 :
THE PROBLEM OF TURNOVER

If you work in a child care program, you've probably encountered staff turnover more often than you wish to remember—maybe even more times than you can count. You know the toll it takes on children, parents and co-workers, not to mention yourself. Some days you may consider it a mild inconvenience. Other days you may want to scream in frustration. You may feel that the problem can't be solved. At times, you may even think about leaving your job, or the entire field of child care, yourself.

The impact of turnover on teaching staff—whether they are new to the field, or have years of experience—is especially profound. For new staff, high turnover at the workplace can easily create a climate of not getting very involved in the job or the center. After all, who needs vision, or a sense of professional career goals, when it seems to be expected that your own ending point could be just around the corner? For experienced staff, nagging questions develop, especially if the job means carrying an extra load every time a new co-worker is hired, but with no reward to show for it: Am I crazy to stay? Am I the only one who cares?

Turnover is demoralizing. It can turn a child care teacher's or director's job into a question of day-to-day survival, rather than a way of working toward high-quality care for children and families. And turnover often has a snowball effect. If one or two key staff members depart, others may also choose to leave, until very quickly, those who remain find that the program is moving

farther away from a vision of good child care, rather than closer to it.

If any of these feelings sounds familiar, we encourage you to keep reading. While this book doesn't hold a magic formula to stem turnover, it does contain a host of ideas to help you make your child care center a place where you and your co-workers can not only stay but continue to grow on the job. Since turnover results from an interplay of many factors, we need multi-faceted solutions to address it. There is no one-size-fits-all approach to turnover, but there is much we can teach and learn from one another as we "take it on."

Every time a caregiver leaves, children experience turnover as loss. Some children, if loss happens often enough, begin to avoid attachments altogether. Parents struggle to reassure their children, but they themselves worry about their children's well-being. The teachers and administrative staff who remain try to juggle the increased responsibilities that turnover adds to their already complex jobs, while at the same time they grapple with their own questions about whether or not to stay. But despite all we have learned and experienced about high staff turnover in child care, and its negative consequences for children and adults, our field has made little progress in reducing it.

A saying from the grassroots Worthy Wage Campaign, which was founded by child care teachers and providers in 1991, not only captures the dilemma we face but hints at a solution:

Parents can't afford to pay

Teachers and providers can't afford to stay

Join us to find a better way.

The slogan acknowledges the financial conflict between families and child care workers in our current child care system. High-quality care, which includes a decent living wage for child care staff, is beyond the reach of most families to pay for alone. But pointing to the conflict also implies a shared solution: parents and child care professionals working together for a vision of child care that doesn't pit their needs against each other. At the Center for the Child Care Workforce, we advocate for a greater investment of public funds targeted to improving child care jobs *and* making care more accessible and affordable to families.

While we recognize that money alone cannot guarantee that teaching staff will stay on the job and continue to grow as professionals, we also know that without more resources, child care programs will be limited in how much they can "take on turnover." But the resources we need will not be easily forthcoming; they will require a large mobilization of stakeholders including parents, child care practitioners, legislators, unions, employers and others who understand the importance of high-quality services for young children. And we believe that discussing the causes and consequences of staff turnover must rise to the top of the agenda within child care programs and throughout the child care field.

DEFINING TURNOVER

As you set out to grapple with the issues raised in this book, some definitions are in order. A great deal of change occurs in child care settings every day, not all of which falls within the scope of this book. As children grow older, they often move from one classroom to another and encounter new teachers. Children come and go as their families move or change jobs, or as they "graduate" to elementary school. Changes also occur in administrative and support staff who do not work as closely with children—and high turnover among administrators and directors is a serious disruption that plagues many programs. This book, however, deals primarily with the most disruptive and potentially troubling form of turnover in child care: the departure of teaching staff.

Because we deal with so much turnover in child care, we tend to view it as all negative, and to think of "stability" or lack of change as all positive.

But sometimes it's better for someone to move on: change can be progress and growth, even when we'd rather avoid it. A center that rarely experiences turnover may be suffering from the equally serious problem of stagnation. We like to distinguish, therefore, between *positive* and *negative turnover*, and *positive* and *negative stability*. Ultimately our goal is to reduce both negative turnover (people leaving the work they love, when they would prefer to stay) and negative stability (people staying, even when they are "burned out" or inappropriate for the job, because they feel they have no better place to go).

There are three main types of teacher turnover in a child care setting:

➡ ***Job turnover*** occurs when a teacher leaves a child care center, but does not necessarily leave the child care field. Job turnover may be involuntary, in the case of a dismissal, or voluntary, as when a teacher leaves a program for a better-paying job or in response to a pregnancy or a family move. Alarm about instability in our field generally centers on job turnover, which is particularly high in child care.

➡ ***Position turnover*** occurs when a teacher moves to a different classroom within a center or to a different site within an agency, resulting from a promotion or perhaps a desire to work with a new age group of children. In this instance, the teacher continues her employment with the center or agency, but in a new role. Position turnover may be disruptive, particularly if it happens too frequently, but it can also provide a stabilizing influence in a program—for example, when children are already somewhat familiar with the person who becomes their new direct caregiver. Position turnover also happens frequently when agencies expand, adding new classrooms or sites to an existing program.

➡ ***Occupational turnover*** occurs when a teacher who leaves a job also departs from the child care field. Most of us can cite many co-workers who have left child care for jobs in other fields such as K-12 education or another related caregiving or service industry. Both job and occupational turnover plague the child care profession. The consequences of job turnover are felt most directly as directors and co-workers struggle to meet ratios in response to a specific staff departure. The effects of occupational turnover surface clearly when there is a shortage of qualified candidates for a job opening, and when it takes a painfully long time to hire a new teacher.

Both *job turnover* and *occupational turnover* require particularly serious attention, and many of the discussions in this workbook apply to either phenomenon.

For a discussion of how to calculate turnover rates in your program, see Part 2, page 59.

WHY STABILIZING THE CHILD CARE WORKFORCE MATTERS: THE CONSEQUENCES OF HIGH TURNOVER

People working in child care describe turnover as a time sponge, an energy drain, or even a plague. Some centers go out of business when turnover gets too high. Parents refer to turnover as a major upheaval in their lives because it disturbs their children and upsets their daily family life; apart from cost, it is the number one child care problem that parents express dissatisfaction about. Employers find their employees distracted and strained when their child care arrangements are disrupted.

Researchers have validated these responses by identifying the detrimental impact of high turnover on child care quality and children's developmental outcomes. The National Child Care Staffing Study revealed that children in centers with high turnover spent less time engaged in social activities, and fewer than one-third engaged in age-appropriate play behaviors with peers. Children in such centers spent more than half the observation time wandering aimlessly around their classrooms. Turnover also affects children's language development; children experiencing high levels of turnover were found to build vocabulary at slower rates than those in more stable settings (Howes, Phillips & Whitebook, 1992; Whitebook et al., 1990).

> **Every time a caregiver leaves, children experience turnover as loss.**

Although the Cost, Quality and Child Outcomes Study, released in 1995, did not report effects on children directly correlated with turnover, it did reveal a similarly strong relationship between child care quality and children's development. Children in higher-quality programs, which were associated with low turnover rates, had more advanced language and pre-math skills. These children also had more positive attitudes toward their child care situation and more positive self-concepts, engaged in better relations with their teachers, and demonstrated more advanced social behavior. The effects of program quality were evident for children from all backgrounds, but children of low-income families were particularly influenced by the quality of their child care arrangements (Helburn, 1995).

We have yet to understand precisely, however, how much and what types of inconsistency children can tolerate in their relationships with caregivers without suffering developmentally. Unlike maternal-child attachment, which is ideally lifelong, a certain degree of caregiver change is inevitable and even desirable. Yet current levels of instability in the child care workforce clearly appear detrimental to children. (See the accompanying article, "Turnover and Attachment," page 28.)

High levels of turnover also place child care centers themselves in jeopardy. Nine years after the original

TURNOVER AND ATTACHMENT:
THE IMPACT ON CHILDREN

"Attachment" refers to the feelings that bind one person to another. A baby leaning toward her mother from someone else's arms, a toddler's face lighting up with joy when his father enters the room, or a preschooler making picture after picture for "Mommy," are all signs of young children's attachment to their parents. When psychologists and educators speak about attachment, they are referring to such behaviors and the feelings they represent, but they also use the term more specifically in accordance with a theory developed by John Bowlby (1969, 1982) and elaborated by other researchers over the past half century (Ainsworth, Blehar, Waters & Wall, 1978). Here, we highlight attachment theory and research as it relates to child care programs and turnover.

WHAT IS ATTACHMENT THEORY?

Attachment theory describes the development of a mental structure, begun during infancy, based on a child's relationship(s) with one or more persons who act as primary caregivers. As the child begins to distinguish her primary caregivers from other people, she seeks contact or closeness with them. This proximity ideally serves to protect the child from physical and psychological harm, and creates a sense of security that permits her to explore her environment.

To develop a healthy attachment, a child must have at least one primary caregiver who is consistent and accessible. Over time, by interacting with primary caregiver(s), the child constructs an internal model of how she and the world of human relationships fit together (Bowlby, 1969, 1982). Although this is done unconsciously, she is assessing whether people and relationships are safe and dependable, or threatening and unreliable (Ainsworth et al., 1978).

Many of us informally observe a child's quality of attachment when we describe her as clinging or aloof with her parents or other caregivers. Psychologists and educators determine whether children are securely, anxiously or insecurely attached to caregivers, using methods of observation that change as children mature and their attachment behaviors (such as seeking contact or signaling distress) become less overt (Waters & Deane, 1985; Main, Kaplan & Cassidy, 1985).

WHY DOES ATTACHMENT MATTER?

Some of the better-known studies of attachment have focused on extreme cases, such as people raised in orphanages who had no childhood opportunities to form attachments with adults, and who continued to have troubled relationships for the rest of their lives. These cases are thankfully uncommon, but there is evidence that milder developmental problems can result when children, for a variety of complex reasons, form insecure or anxious attachments to their parents (Bretherton, 1985; van IJzendoorn, Sagi & Lambermon, 1992). Children who were anxiously attached to their mothers as infants, for example, have been found to function more poorly in preschool than children who were securely attached; to be highly dependent, non-compliant and poorly skilled in social interaction with their peers; and to be described by teachers as hostile, impulsive, prone to give up easily, and withdrawn (Erickson, Sroufe & Egeland, 1985).

HOW DOES ATTACHMENT THEORY
APPLY TO CHILDREN AND THEIR TEACHERS?

Because disturbances in attachment do affect children's development, researchers have spent many years examining whether child care undermines a child's primary relationship to her parents or guardians. In stark contrast to children in poorly-run orphanages, children in child care centers do have a primary attachment to their parents, and with few exceptions, researchers today agree that child care does not disturb these relationships (Belsky & Cassidy, 1994). Children with poor attachments to their mothers, however, are at higher risk developmentally if they attend poor-quality child care programs with unskilled caregivers and high turnover (Kontos, 1992; Lynch & Cicchetti, 1992; van IJzendoorn et al., 1992). If they attend high-quality care, however, secure attachments to teachers can compensate for insecure attachments to their parents (Howes & Hamilton, 1992a, 1992b, 1993; Howes & Matheson, 1992).

In more recent interpretations of attachment theory, child care teachers and providers have come into focus for their positive role as available, responsive adults who can help children build an internal image of the world as safe and of themselves as lovable and valuable. Children's relationships with teachers and providers differ in intensity and form from those with their parents or primary caregivers, but can be similarly classified as secure or insecure (Howes & Matheson, 1992; van IJzendoorn et al., 1992; Goossens & van IJzendoorn, 1991; Anderson, Nagle, Roberts & Smith, 1981). Children are more likely to be securely attached to their teachers if they attend classrooms where teachers are highly responsive and involved with them, rather than harsh or detached. Teachers with these qualities are also more likely to be in programs with low turnover. Children securely attached to teachers have been found to be more competent with their peers, less hesitant, and more likely to engage with their teachers (Howes et al., 1992; Howes & Hamilton, 1992a).

WHAT DOES RESEARCH TELL US ABOUT TURNOVER AND OTHER DISRUPTIONS IN CHILDREN'S RELATIONSHIPS WITH TEACHERS?

Like other forms of attachment, teacher-child relationships require some degree of stability to develop and strengthen, but we do not yet know precisely how resilient they are to change. Howes and Hamilton (1993) differentiated among types of change in child care programs, and their impact on children's relationships with teachers and peers. Over three years, they observed 72 children who experienced an average of 2.4 changes in primary teachers, with 44 percent of children experiencing three or more changes. When children faced more changes, they were rated as lower in gregarious behaviors (laughing, running, etc.) and higher in social withdrawal and aggression. Children who experienced more primary teacher changes over the course of the study were more likely to be aggressive toward others as four-year-olds. Younger children were the most vulnerable to changes in their primary caregivers.

HOW CAN POSITIVE TEACHER-CHILD ATTACHMENTS BE PROMOTED?

The first step is retaining skilled teachers, who can help children re-establish a secure relationship or switch from an insecure to a secure one. But to do so, teachers must know how to interact with and supervise children in a sensitive, age-appropriate manner; they must know how to create developmentally enhancing environments for children; and they must have sufficient support—including decent job conditions that encourage them to stay in the child care field. ★

National Child Care Staffing Study, 30 percent of the original sample of 226 centers were closed. These centers as a group had reported much higher levels of staff turnover when the original data were collected in 1988 (54 versus 38 percent) than the centers that remained open in 1997. In the centers that later closed, 41 percent of teaching staff had been on the job for a year or less in 1988 (vs. 28 percent in centers that remained open). The centers that closed had also paid lower wages, and had hired staff with more limited educational backgrounds, than those that remained open (Whitebook et al., 1990, 1998).

In our study of centers seeking NAEYC accreditation in three California communities between 1994 and 1996, the Center for the Child Care Workforce found that turnover played an important role in determining not only which centers were successful at achieving accreditation, but also which of the accredited centers provided good quality (as opposed to mediocre) care. The centers that were least successful at becoming accredited reported higher rates of turnover. Among the accredited centers, those that achieved higher levels of quality paid their teachers more and retained more of their highly-skilled staff (Whitebook, Sakai & Howes, 1997).

What's most clear is that a very difficult-to-break cycle operates in the child care field. Centers that pay the lowest salaries typically attract teaching staff who have completed less specialized child care training, and are least likely to provide appropriate caregiving. These staff are also most likely to leave their jobs—primarily as a result of poor pay, and also, perhaps, because the job of caring for a group of young children is significantly more difficult without proper preparation. It is difficult to determine to what extent lower quality in child care stems from the direct impact of turnover events themselves, and to what extent it stems from high-turnover centers employing staff with lower levels of education, training and skill. It is likely that the link between high turnover and low quality is an interplay of these factors.

> Experienced teachers start to ask: Am I crazy to stay? Am I the only one who cares?

TURNOVER IN PERSPECTIVE: CHILD CARE AND OTHER INDUSTRIES

All industries wrestle with employee turnover. Depending on the type of product or service it provides and the wage level of its employees, every business will tend to define a certain level of turnover as normal and acceptable. But while employers generally expect more turnover in low-wage industries, it is problematic to tolerate high turnover in a human service occupation such as child care, where it can have such a negative impact on the young children we serve. When turn-

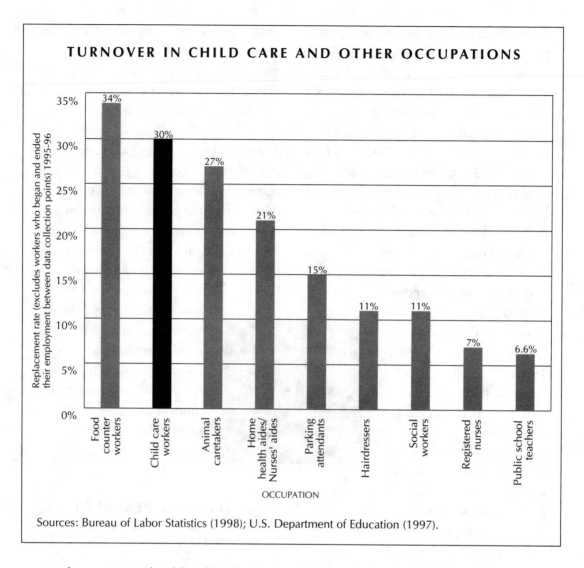

TURNOVER IN CHILD CARE AND OTHER OCCUPATIONS

Replacement rate (excludes workers who began and ended their employment between data collection points) 1995-96

- Food counter workers: 34%
- Child care workers: 30%
- Animal caretakers: 27%
- Home health aides/Nurses' aides: 21%
- Parking attendants: 15%
- Hairdressers: 11%
- Social workers: 11%
- Registered nurses: 7%
- Public school teachers: 6.6%

OCCUPATION

Sources: Bureau of Labor Statistics (1998); U.S. Department of Education (1997).

over becomes intolerable, all industries start examining strategies for increasing the retention of their workforce.

How does the turnover situation in child care compare to other occupations—particularly those with similar pay rates, client needs and job qualifications? Is it getting worse or improving? Answering these questions can put child care turnover in perspective, and help to frame our discussions with policy makers, employers and others whose support we need in order to sta-

bilize the child care workforce.

In fact, job turnover among center-based child care teaching staff in the United States has reached crisis proportions, with roughly one in three child care workers leaving the job each year—approximately twice as high as turnover in the average U.S. company, and far exceeding the turnover rate in other U.S. educational settings.

Back in 1977, the annual turnover rate among child care teachers and assistants was only 15 percent, with 40 percent of centers reporting no turnover (Coelen, Glantz & Calore, 1979). But little more than a decade later, the National Child Care Staffing Study (NCCSS) (Whitebook et al., 1990) reported a 41-percent annual turnover rate for center-based teaching staff, and all but seven percent of the 225 programs in the study reported some turnover in the previous year. Another multi-city examination conducted in 1992-1993, the Cost, Quality and Child Outcomes Study (Helburn, 1995), found a similar annual turnover rate of 37 percent for teaching staff, distributed across all but 12 percent of the 401 centers in the study.*

A 1997 follow-up to the National Child Care Staffing Study (Whitebook et al., 1998) showed that this disturbing pattern has continued. Even in this study's relatively high-quality sample of centers, roughly one-quarter of teachers and two-fifths of assistant teachers left their jobs each year, for an overall turnover rate of 31 percent—and twenty percent of centers reported teaching staff turnover rates of *50 percent a year or more*. Only one-third of the teaching staff in these centers had been at their current jobs for five years or more, and only 14 percent of them were at their centers when the first study data were gathered in 1988.

---

* Turnover rates among relatives and family child care providers likewise hovered around forty percent per year, although just over a third of non-regulated care providers and fewer than half of relatives interviewed by Kontos, Howes, Shinn and Galinsky (1995) continued to provide care one year after the initial contact.

By contrast, the turnover rates in 1995-96—the most recent year for which data are available—were 6.6 percent for all public school teachers, 3.1 percent for public kindergarten teachers, and 16 percent for private kindergarten teachers (U.S. Department of Education, 1997). The U.S. Department of Labor's Bureau of Labor Statistics tracks turnover rates across industries by identifying a group of employees at one point in time and then returning a year later to see whether they hold the same positions. This method of data collection, unfortunately, fails to capture those workers who might have come and gone between the data collection points—a number which can be substantial in child care.

Although turnover is now more widespread in child care than it was twenty years ago, it is still concentrated in certain types of programs and among staff with certain characteristics. Among full-day center-based programs, those which are operated on a non-profit basis and/or receive greater public or corporate subsidies have generally lower turnover than for-profit programs (Whitebook et al., 1998; Helburn, 1995; Whitebook, Phillips & Howes, 1993; Whitebook et al., 1990). Public school pre-K and Head Start programs, which typically operate half-day for nine to ten months per year, also report relatively lower levels of teacher turnover (Willer et al., 1991).

Teachers—defined as staff who are responsible for a group of children and

TURNOVER AND STABILITY
BY AUSPICE AND ACCREDITATION STATUS

Program Type	Annual Turnover: All Teaching Staff	Annual Turnover: Teachers Only	Annual Turnover: Assistant Teachers Only	Percentage of Teaching Staff Remaining 5 to 10 Years	Percentage of Teaching Staff Remaining 10 Years or More
Independent For-Profit	35%	27%	59%	29%	13%
For-Profit Chain	45%	42%	54%	20%	8%
Independent Nonprofit	28%	27%	34%	39%	18%
Church-Related Nonprofit	26%	20%	33%	29%	11%
NAEYC Accredited	20%	15%	38%	53%	26%
Non-NAEYC Accredited	34%	29%	40%	29%	12%
All Centers	31%	27%	39%	32%	14%

Source: Whitebook et al. (1998)

often have adult supervisory duties—tend to remain on the job longer than the aides and assistants they oversee.* The most rapid turnover tends to occur among the least qualified staff, who typically have received little or no college-level education or specialized early childhood training (Helburn, 1995; Whitebook et al., 1990). There is some indication, however, that new

teaching opportunities in elementary education, fueled by school reforms such as class size reduction and by a recent increase in the birth rate, are drawing a high number of teachers with college degrees in early childhood education away from child care jobs (Whitebook, Burton, Montgomery, Hikido & Chambers, 1996). In addition, replacement child care teaching staff tend to be less well-educated and trained than their predecessors (Whitebook et al., 1990), and are among the most likely to leave their

* Similarly, among family child care providers, those who are more likely to continue providing care are regulated, report higher estimated income, and receive more informal training than non-regulated care providers or children's relatives (Kontos et al., 1995).

jobs soon (Whitebook et al., 1993). The challenge facing the child care industry, therefore, involves not only minimizing turnover in general, but maximizing stability among the more skilled and experienced members of the workforce.

Some economists and policy makers view the high rate of turnover in child care as an inevitable consequence of a low-paying industry, one that is dominated by women in their child-bearing years who face relatively minimal training and education requirements. Because mothers of young children typically move in and out of the workforce, and because many presumably choose to work in child care in order to address their own child care needs, high turnover in child care is sometimes viewed as inevitable. But as comparisons to other industries show, child care staff turnover is very high even among low-paying, female-dominated occupations.

UNDERSTANDING WHY TEACHERS LEAVE

Across industries, theorists identify three main determinants of employee retention and turnover within a work site: compensation, organizational climate, and hiring practices (Greengard, 1995; White, 1995; Mercer, 1998).

Compensation

It is generally agreed that retention is maximized when employees receive wages and benefits that are equal to or greater than the average for jobs in similar workplaces with similar requirements (Stivison, 1992; Mobley, 1982). But when an entire industry is characterized by low wages, employers who offer competitive compensation packages can still face undesirably high turnover (Kim, in press; Parker & Rhine, 1991). As a result, child care centers may often need to exceed the average compensation package in the community, not just match it, in order to attract and retain staff—especially those with a high level of training and skill (Powell, Montgomery & Cosgrove, 1994).

Work environment

Adequate pay and benefits, while necessary, are not sufficient; the work environment or organizational climate also contributes to the level of turnover and stability in a work setting (Anderson, 1982; James & Jones, 1974; Taguiri, 1978). The climate involves the extent to which interpersonal relations are satisfying, roles and lines of authority are clearly delineated, and employees feel comfortable in expressing their needs (Steele & Jenks, 1997). Also included here would be the extent to which workers are able to participate in decision-making and management, workers' input is heard and valued, and the organization's problem-solving process results in positive solutions. Bloom (1996), whose work focuses on child care settings, identifies the dimensions of organizational climate as:

✓ collegiality,

ACTIVITY

RATE THE REASONS FOR TURNOVER

Think about the people you know who no longer work at your center or in the child care field, or consider why you left your last child care job. Then fill out the following chart.

How much do you think turnover resulted from:

REASON	A GREAT DEAL	SOMEWHAT	NOT MUCH
Low pay			
Relationships with co-workers			
The skill level of co-workers			
The director's skill level			
Lack of benefits			
Poor working conditions, e.g., no breaks, no staff room			
Lack of financial rewards for investing in more training and education			
Low social status of child care work			
The nature of the work itself; burn-out			
Family issues, e.g., new baby, relocation			
Turnover of co-workers			
Lack of respect from administrator/director			
Lack of respect from parents			
Poor hiring decision			
Insufficient training			
Other			

RATE THE REASONS FOR TURNOVER
(continued from previous page)

Use this exercise to assess your own current thinking about the causes of turnover. Then try it again in the future to gauge any changes in your thinking that may have occurred as you worked with others on turnover issues.

This is also an effective exercise to try in a group. You can use it as an ice-breaker to get people thinking about their own and others' attitudes about why turnover happens in child care. Place large signs reading "a great deal," "somewhat" and "not much" at different points in the room. Ask one person to read the list of possible reasons for turnover, and for each item, ask the others to move to the sign that best matches their opinion. Notice which items cause a nearly unanimous stampede, which ones create a major split or disagreement, and which ones people find it hard to decide about. If you do this activity with co-workers, these similarities and differences will give you important information as you start discussing how to reduce turnover in your center. What seem to be the major causes that most people agree on? Which areas is the group divided about?

✓ professional growth,

✓ supervisor support,

✓ the clarity of rules and authority,

✓ the reward system,

✓ decision making,

✓ goal consensus,

✓ task orientation,

✓ the physical setting, and

✓ the degree of emphasis on innovation.

Adults derive satisfaction from environments that provide interesting, meaningful and challenging work; the opportunity to use all of their capabilities; recognition and respect for their achievements; the presence of congenial colleagues; and having control over and taking responsibility for their work. When any of these are lacking, dissatisfaction can result, and especially in child care, this feeling can be compounded by low wages, poor benefits, and/or inadequate sick days and vacation time.

Hiring practices

The extent to which an employer makes a positive match between an individual and a particular job is associated with the level of stability in a workplace (Balfour & Neff, 1993). Much turnover, it is argued, results from hiring the wrong person for the job. In industries such as child care, this is a particularly serious problem for

CHILD CARE WORKFORCE EARNINGS IN PERSPECTIVE

A comparison of median hourly wages between child care jobs and other occupations*

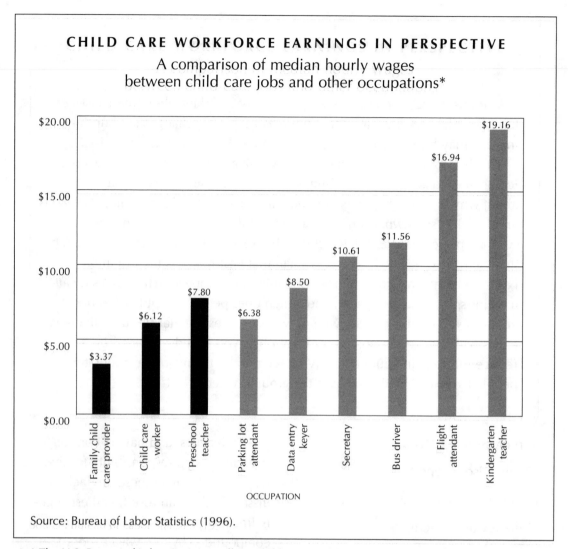

OCCUPATION

Source: Bureau of Labor Statistics (1996).

* The U.S. Bureau of Labor Statistics collects child care workforce data through numerous surveys, using a variety of occupational titles. Center-based staff are classified either as preschool teachers or as child care workers, unfortunately creating a misleading division of the workforce, when in fact most teaching staff, regardless of title, take part in both educational and caregiving duties. For more discussion of these issues, see Center for the Child Care Workforce, 1998b.

two intertwined reasons. First, the work itself cannot be put "on hold": there is often an immediate need to hire a staff replacement, because the center must meet legally mandated adult-child ratios. Second, the minimal qualifications for child care jobs, combined with often minimal job rewards, can create a pool of applicants who do not have adequate preparation or inclination to do the work well. This leads to the "warm body" syndrome: hiring someone to ensure sufficient staffing in a classroom, even when it may be clear from the start that the new person will contribute little to (or even detract from) the caregiving environment.

Depending on the industry, there

WHY ARE CHILD CARE WORKERS SO UNDERPAID?

Whether you feel that wages are the primary cause of turnover, or only one of many reasons why people leave their jobs, understanding the reasons why child care workers are underpaid can help direct you toward solutions. Part of the reason is the persistence of attitudes about women's work as unskilled, and the fact that many people are not used to paying for caregiving services. The care of young children is also generally seen as the personal responsibility of individual families, not as a social concern.

But two other economic reasons also underlie the problem. First, child care is a labor-intensive industry. This means that staffing costs are the biggest expenditure in a child care budget, because this type of service requires a high number of staff, and the expenditure is high even when staff are underpaid. Compared to elementary or secondary classroom settings, many more staff are needed to care for younger children, especially infants and toddlers.

But this is only part of the problem: the second issue is how child care revenues are generated. Most come from parent fees, and most parents are limited in how much they can pay. And even though child care costs a lot from a family's perspective, what parents can afford does not necessarily result in sufficient wages for staff—particularly if the center is also expected to generate a profit. Child care, in fact, is the only educational service relying so heavily on parents to foot the bill, with parent fees accounting for 60 percent of the national expenditure on child care. By contrast, parents contribute only about one-fourth of higher education costs, with government and philanthropy assuming the remaining burden (Mitchell, Stoney & Dichter, 1997). If public and private funds beyond parent fees were available for child care, at reimbursement rates that truly allowed programs to offer quality services, and with funds particularly targeted to retaining a skilled and stable workforce, our child care staffing crisis could come to an end. ★

will be a different balance among the causes of turnover. In child care, research has repeatedly identified low wages as the driving force behind turnover—not surprisingly, given how child care compensation compares to that in other industries (see chart on page 38). In addition, most child care workers do not receive health or retirement benefits, and in many settings, they receive few if any paid sick days, holidays or vacation days. Many child care teachers work several unpaid hours each week in classroom planning, staff or parent meetings, cleanup and other activities. Adding insult to this situation, there is often little finan-cial reward for investing in one's professional development to become a better teacher. An enormous responsibility is placed in child care teachers' hands, but their paychecks fail to reflect either the value of the service they perform or the skill it requires to

TOP TEN REASONS (OTHER THAN COMPENSATION) WHY TEACHERS WANT TO QUIT
"an unscientific survey"

1. Having to arrange your own substitute when you're sick, or to take a vacation day.

2. Being asked to perform other tasks, including clean-up, during class-room planning and preparation time.

3. Finding that some staff are in the information loop and others are not.

4. Seeing your most skilled and experienced co-workers leaving child care to work in a supermarket or a parking lot.

5. Having to buy or contribute your own classroom supplies because the center doesn't have enough.

6. Being expected to attend evening or weekend family activities at the center, or to work extra hours, without pay (a practice which is usual-ly illegal).

7. Secrecy about salaries, so that it's hard to judge whether you are being treated fairly, or receiving different pay for the same educational background and level of responsibility.

8. Having your work partner or classroom assignment changed without notice or input.

9. A director who "fills in" in the classroom occasionally, but without letting go of the director role.

10. A job description that ends with the words, "and other duties as assigned." ★

do their jobs well. The combination is a recipe for high turnover.

Yet higher wages alone will not guarantee that people will stay on the job or that they will provide high-quality child care. In our recent study of NAEYC-accredited centers, the Center for the Child Care Workforce examined a variety of workplace and staff characteristics to determine which of these might be predictors for retaining highly-skilled teaching staff. Not surprisingly, the skilled teachers who remained worked in centers rated higher in quality than others in their community. We also found that teachers who were rated as providing sensitive, developmentally appropriate care were more likely to remain on the job if:

➡ they earned higher-than-average wages (approximately $2.00 more per hour than highly-skilled teachers who had left the job)

and

➡ they worked in a center where other highly-skilled teachers, as well as the director, also remained on the job.

These findings suggest that, just as a climate of high turnover tends to beget more turnover, a climate of stability begets more stability. Teachers want to work with other well-trained colleagues who, as a team, establish a rewarding adult environment as well as a stable caregiving situation for children (Whitebook, Sakai & Howes, 1997). Researchers have also found that although child care teachers often move into administrative positions to earn better salaries, they generally would prefer being better paid as *teachers*, and remain working directly with children in the classroom (Burton, Whitebook, Sakai, Babula & Haack, 1994).

Teachers themselves often acknowledge other causes of turnover besides wages. Sometimes, very practical issues push people "over the edge." In one center, teachers identified the shortage of adult bathrooms (one stall for 70 people) as a major workplace problem—but this issue only surfaced when the teachers and director began developing a plan to reduce turnover in their center. Recently, a group of teachers and assistants participating in our training series on turnover created a "top ten" list of reasons other than compensation that make them consider leaving their jobs (see page 40). Although the list was partly created tongue-in-cheek, we found that it drew few laughs when we shared it at other training events; many people found it all too "close to home."

DIRECTORS AND TURNOVER

"See Joyce, the director, with her head in her hands. See the tears in her eyes. See the scream forming inside her. See all the names crossed off her substitute list. In the last six months, Joyce has had to find four new teachers. How will she ever be able to reassure the parents in Sonja's room, now that Sonja too is leaving?"

The fictional character Joyce in the ABC Child Care Center story (page 12) captures the experience of many directors. A good number of tears fell at our training events, too, as directors shared their frustrations about turnover—above all, how it kept them from attending to the many other tasks involved in running a high-quality program. Many directors felt that they faced a growing list of urgent items to deal with, but could rarely get beyond just trying to keep their programs fully staffed. Repeatedly, they mentioned

---

TOP TEN REASONS
(OTHER THAN TEACHER TURNOVER)
WHY DIRECTORS WANT TO QUIT

1. Being "on call" at any hour of the day—leading to the feeling that you can never take a break, a sick day or a vacation.

2. The scope and diversity of responsibilities (or, the "not-enough-hours-in-a-day" syndrome).

3. Being squeezed in too many directions by people with competing needs: parents, staff, the board of directors or center owners, and the community.

4. Wanting to be a learner, not just a knower, but never feeling that there is time or opportunity for your own professional growth.

5. Inadequate compensation and lack of benefits—especially retirement benefits—for yourself and the rest of the staff.

6. Feeling like the "mom"—having to be everything to everybody, with no boundaries.

7. Having to implement unpopular decisions, or deal with a difficult employee.

8. Lack of support from above, whether it is a board of directors, funding agency, executive director, or owner. (It is increasingly common for child care center directors to be mid-level managers, rather than the ultimate authority in the workplace.)

9. Inadequate training for the complexity of responsibilities.

10. Never a quiet moment to finish a project without interruption, and few opportunities to appreciate your accomplishments. ★

---

how isolated and overloaded they felt.

In exploring turnover issues among directors, two solutions emerged. First, many directors realized from talking to each other that a director support group was essential—not a luxury to pursue at some later point when things had gotten more "under control." As they talked specifically about such problems as hiring new staff or arranging subs, they heard new ideas, had their feelings validated, and came to recognize each other as sources of expert help.

Second, directors began to reflect upon their own comments and to recognize the extent to which they saw turnover as their problem to solve alone—rather than a shared problem that teaching staff, parents, board members and others also had a stake in solving. Many directors spend an enormous amount of time and energy trying to "take on turnover" single-handedly, only to be disappointed when their efforts are unappreciated or unsuccessful. As we discuss in more depth in Part 3, creating an atmosphere of hon-

ACTIVITY

CREATING YOUR OWN TOP TEN LIST

Now, make a list of the top ten things in your workplace that make you the most frustrated. There are several ways to do this:

✓ on your own, to clarify your own priorities for change,

✓ with co-workers in your program, to learn what frustrates others, and

✓ with other practitioners in your community, to generate a priority list for advocacy efforts.

If you are a director, try also creating a list of what you think makes teaching staff want to quit. Similarly, teaching staff can try developing a list of what frustrates the director. Then share these lists with each other to gain a better understanding of each other's needs and how everyone might provide better mutual support.

If relationships are strained in your center, however, this exercise might not be a good place to start, because it requires a level of trust that may not exist. Another, less threatening approach is to ask everyone to write down one or two things they like about working at the center, and one or two things they do not like. Everyone can then put these into a bowl and take turns reading the responses. In this way, "who wrote what" is somewhat more disguised, but it can still help to get the most pressing issues at your center "on the table."

est communication among staff about turnover and other problems—and sharing decision-making power—can ease the isolation and sense of burden that many directors feel.

Directors at our turnover training events decided that they needed a "top ten" list of their own (see page 42).

∎ ∎ ∎

The remainder of *Taking On Turnover* is devoted to three different types of turnover planning:

➡ turnover *management* plans (how to cope better with turnover whenever it occurs in your program), discussed in Part 2;

➡ turnover *reduction* plans (how to work toward preventing or reducing turnover in your program), discussed in Part 3; and

➡ turnover *action* plans (how to join with others in your program and in the wider community to reduce turnover throughout the child care profession), discussed in Part 4.

Improving compensation, hiring practices and the organizational climate are the keys to reducing turnover in many industries (see Part 3). But before tackling such longer-term issues, employers in many industries begin with two other strategies.

The first is to calculate turnover costs within a given organization, and to determine how dollars spent on turnover could be redirected to address staff retention. The second, closely related to the first, involves identifying the best practices for "managing turnover" as smoothly as possible whenever it occurs. Some of the strategies an organization uses when faced with a turnover event may ease the transition, but others may worsen its negative effects and undermine the quality of one's products or services. These issues of turnover costs, and the best practices for managing turnover and reducing the stress it causes for children, parents and staff, are discussed in the following chapter.

Part 2:

ASSESSING AND MANAGING THE EFFECTS OF TURNOVER

Our long-term goal must be to reduce turnover drastically in the child care field, because it has become unacceptably high. But we must also recognize that some measure of turnover is inevitable in any workplace. It can even be a positive change. A staff member may be leaving to advance her education, or to work with a different age group, or to move with her family to a new place. She may have reached the decision that she is not well-suited to child care, and wants to pursue another kind of work.

But even when it comes about for positive reasons—and especially when it is disappointing or traumatic—a staff departure affects the children and adults who remain. Children may find it harder to separate from their parents in the morning. Children and parents alike can feel disoriented and anxious to see new faces and miss familiar ones. Teachers often work twice as hard to keep a classroom running smoothly, and to keep curriculum planning and implementation on-track. Administrators often feel overburdened with the job of finding a qualified replacement.

At times, your center may experience too much change at once. At other times, the opposite might be true. And as we have already noted, "stability" or lack of change can be a negative quality in a child care program if it leads to dull routines and an absence of growth. Although you may not be able to totally control change, there are ways to cope with it more consciously and intentionally, to plan for it, and to minimize its negative effects. If we

handle turnover poorly, or avoid responding in a timely way, we can make it worse, so that it begets more turnover, creating a situation in which other staff also decide to leave.

Knowing that some degree of turnover will always take place in a child care center, how can we manage it more effectively, and ease the disruption and harm it can cause? How can we create more stability for children, and reduce stress for teachers, administrators and parents?

Consider these fairly typical scenarios of turnover events:

Scenario One

Since a new director, Sharon, was hired two years ago, several assistant teachers have left the Sunshine Child Care Center, but fortunately, the head teachers in all four classrooms have remained on the job. Two weeks ago, however, Lisa, the head teacher in the toddler room, announced that she would be leaving in six weeks because her husband is being transferred. Today,

Pam, the head teacher in one of the preschool classrooms, had to tell the director that she has accepted a job teaching kindergarten at the local public school starting in two weeks. She had been about to make an announcement at the last staff meeting, but when Lisa said she was leaving, she couldn't bring herself to say anything. Financially, however, she doesn't know what else to do. She still has college loans to repay, and the school district will underwrite most of the cost of earning her teaching credential. She will also earn $5-6,000 more per year, plus benefits, and work ten months per year instead of twelve.

Scenario Two

During the past two years, Twin Oaks Child Care Center experienced more than its share of turnover. Theresa, the director, who has been at the center for ten years, faced a serious challenge as four out of seven teachers in the infant rooms, two of the five toddler teachers, and five of the 10 preschool teachers all left. There was nearly 100% turnover among assistants and aides. This year has been much better. The center has been able to improve its salaries and benefits, and many of the new staff have been participating in on-site training. Most of the newly-hired teachers and assistants have worked well together. But despite all this progress, Theresa now has to immediately terminate a new head teacher, Mary, for using

abusive language toward a parent. Mary believes that she is being treated unfairly, and has made her feelings clear to the entire staff, four or five of whom seem to be taking her side. A meeting of the center's board of directors is scheduled to take place three nights from now. The situation is very tense.

In the first scenario, turnover is happening largely because of positive changes in the teachers' lives— although the issue of low pay in child care is a strong consideration for at least one of them. Scenario (2) illustrates the fact that even if you have done your best to prevent turnover by addressing pay, staff development and other issues, it will still happen sometimes—even the trauma of having to dismiss a staff member. In both of these situations, there are programmatic, financial, personal and emotional changes to manage. And the various people involved—the children and parents, the departing and remaining staff members, the director, the board of directors, any substitutes that work at the center during the transition, and the newly hired replacement staff—have a wide variety of needs.

In scenario (1), a number of questions arise:

➠ How will the changes be communicated to parents, staff, the board and the children?

➠ How will the teaching staff be included in planning and in hiring new staff?

ACTIVITY

QUESTIONS FOR DISCUSSION

Think about the last time turnover happened at your center, and consider the following questions, either on your own or as a group discussion at a staff meeting.

✓ What was the hardest thing for you about losing a fellow staff member?

✓ How did it change your job?

✓ How did you cope?

✓ What were the financial costs?

✓ What added responsibilities did you have, if any?

✓ Which tasks were left undone?

✓ How did the children respond?

✓ Which practices, if any, helped the children and parents cope with the change?

✓ What would you do differently next time?

➠ Is it possible to hire a head teacher from within the pool of assistant teachers at the center?

➠ What are everyone's added responsibilities?

➠ What are the added costs?

➠ Are short-term or long-term substitute teachers available, and is there an ongoing process for recruiting them?

➠ How can the center address concerns about teachers' needs for advancement and higher pay, to minimize their need to seek better-paying teaching jobs elsewhere?

➠ What activities will help children say "goodbye" and "hello"?

➠ How will the center handle supervision issues for the remaining assistant teachers, and orientation for the new head teachers?

➠ What kinds of support are available for the director, who has only been on the job for two years?

For scenario (2), many of these same questions still apply, but with the added difficulties of a tense and mistrustful atmosphere:

➠ How will the dismissal be discussed with the staff, board and parents?

➡ What are the confidentiality issues that restrict how much can be talked about?

➡ What documentation is needed?

➡ What is the role of the child care licensing agency?

➡ Are false rumors spreading about why Mary was dismissed?

➡ How can Mary be assured of being treated fairly?

➡ Can an outside facilitator or other person help the staff with conflict resolution?

➡ What will the children be told, and, especially if Mary had to leave abruptly, how will they "say good-bye"?

➡ Having made significant progress on staff development and other issues in the past year, how can the center use all this groundwork as a strength to build upon?

Later in this chapter, we'll return to a number of these issues in more detail. Meanwhile, try the activity on page 47 to reflect on how you and your center have responded to turnover.

THE PROCESS OF CHANGE: PERSONAL STYLES AND NEEDS

Change is a highly personal experience. People react in a wide variety of ways to change of any kind. Some of us tend to feel very skeptical or fearful, and try to hold onto familiar objects or routines for a sense of comfort. Some will feel harried, or overburdened, or angry; some will deny as long as possible that it is even happening. Others reach out and embrace change, and seem to transform themselves or their surroundings constantly. None of these orientations is right or wrong, and there is probably little we can do to change our basic responses to change—they are often emotional and unpredictable, and not necessarily rational. But before we can help children deal with change, we have to know ourselves and the ways we tend to face it—because these will color how, for better or worse, we deal with the changes that come with turnover.

> Before we can help children deal with change, we have to know ourselves and the ways we tend to face it.

Even small changes can have big effects, and even positive changes can be stressful, such as revamping a classroom, moving to a new site, or welcoming a new set of children and families to the program. Large or small, change can be associated with relief and excitement, or with a sense of disruption or loss.

This is especially true for children. As we noted in Part 1, researchers studying the quality of child care arrangements have highlighted children's need for continuity and stability in their relationships with adults and peers. To gain the confidence they need to grow and learn, children must develop a sense of trust in the people and environments that make up their world. (At the same time, we should remember that children are changing all the time, and tend to be more resilient and adaptable than adults.) During times of staff turnover and other transitions, children will typically need to:

- be informed in an age-appropriate manner

- have their feelings about the change acknowledged, discussed and honored

- say good-bye to the departing person

- trust that daily routines and other aspects of the child care environment will remain consistent and predictable

- have their relationship with the new staff person facilitated, but not rushed or forced.

A different set of issues will come up for adults as a result of a staff departure. It is normal for all of us to move back and forth among various responses to change and disruption. The "powerless" or "victim"-oriented response might be to ask, "Why me? How can this be happening again?" The "critic" may declare, "Turnover has been a huge disruption in the past and it's going to be the same way again." The "bystander" might think, "If I ignore this situation the fuss will die down and the problem will go away—or maybe the more experienced people will take care of it." The "optimist" may decide, "This change could be an opportunity to improve some things

about our workplace."

In spite of different personal styles, staff will need to:

- communicate, be informed, and express concerns about the change

- be involved in developing a plan to deal with the change, and with future turnover situations—contributing their expertise about how the classrooms function on a daily basis, and what the staffing patterns and needs are

- have a series of policies in place that clarify staff relationships and procedures

- say good-bye to the departing person

- integrate the new staff member and build new team relationships.

What do program administrators need when turnover occurs? They go through many of same feelings as other staff, but as leaders, they may not always feel able to show them. As a result, fellow administrators or friends may be important sources of support. Administrators need to:

- set a climate of grappling with issues of turnover and change openly and calmly

- enlist staff feedback, support and help in planning and decision-making

- say good-bye to the departing person

- seek out peer support from other directors/administrators

- seek out training or other ways to increase their management skills

- relieve any feelings of isolation that may develop.

Finally, parents have their own set of needs when turnover happens. Above all, they may want reassurance that basic routines, activities and other aspects of the program will remain consistent and reliable for their children. Parents need to:

- be informed of upcoming changes, and have an opportunity to express concerns

- know about the center's overall recruitment and hiring policies, preferably outlined in a parent handbook that they receive when enrolling a child

- say good-bye to the departing person

- be introduced to substitutes and newly-hired staff

- have opportunities to tell the new staff person about their child

- feel welcome to ask questions, express concerns, and/or help out in the classroom or in other ways during the transition period.

CHECKLISTS

ASSESS HOW YOUR CENTER RESPONDS TO TURNOVER

Try using the following checklists to assess your current practices in responding to turnover, and to identify priority areas for improvement. This activity was developed with the help of 40 teachers and 20 directors participating in a training series on managing turnover.

Helping Children Cope With Turnover

Consistent caregiving is essential to children's healthy development. Keep in mind, too, that like adults, children have very different temperaments and responses to change, and will not all have the same needs when turnover happens.

	We currently do this	This is a priority to work on	Not a priority at this time
➡ COMMUNICATING ABOUT THE CHANGE			
Inform children when a staff person is leaving, and if or when they will return.	❑	❑	❑
Explain to children in an age-appropriate manner why the staff person is leaving and/or will not be returning.	❑	❑	❑
Provide sufficient lead time, if possible, for children to accustom themselves to the news, but not further in advance than they can understand.	❑	❑	❑
Share your feelings with the children about this change, as a way of modeling for them how to show and share their own.	❑	❑	❑
Provide opportunities for children to talk about the teacher who is leaving, and/or to write letters or make pictures. For example, ask them to make a list of the special things they like or will miss about this teacher. Perhaps they can create a story, video or "mural" (on a large roll of paper).	❑	❑	❑
Use a calendar to mark the days remaining before the teacher will leave or the days prior to her return.	❑	❑	❑

Helping Children Cope With Turnover
continued

	We currently do this	This is a priority to work on	Not a priority at this time
Provide an opportunity for the teacher to say good-bye. If this is not possible, be sure that children at least have the chance to talk about this change.	❑	❑	❑
Create a ceremony to mark the transition and provide closure.	❑	❑	❑
Include discussion and materials about change as a regular part of the curriculum, not just as something to talk about when a big change is occurring.	❑	❑	❑
Encourage departing teachers, when appropriate, to send occasional cards or come to visit.	❑	❑	❑

Add your own suggestions:

➡ INTEGRATING NEW PEOPLE

Inform children whenever possible that they will be having a substitute.	❑	❑	❑
Introduce substitutes to children, and make sure that the substitute knows the children's names. For example, use a picture board with children's and staff members' pictures and names as a reference, or give the children name tags if necessary.	❑	❑	❑
Use in-house or long-term substitutes whenever possible.	❑	❑	❑
Enlist the children's help in orienting the substitute to the room—for example, by giving her a tour of the classroom, or explaining the sequence of daily routines.	❑	❑	❑

Helping Children Cope With Turnover
continued

	We currently do this	This is a priority to work on	Not a priority at this time
Try to arrange no less than one week's overlap between the departing and new staff person whenever possible. (This is especially important for infants who are sensitive to unfamiliar faces.) If overlap isn't possible, have the new teacher observe at least once before she begins employment.	❑	❑	❑
Ask the departing or continuing teacher to introduce the new teacher to the children. When possible, prepare children for her arrival.	❑	❑	❑
Minimize potential conflict situations during the first few days for new teachers. (For example, avoid having the new teacher take primary responsibility for potty training as her first interaction with toddlers.)	❑	❑	❑
Allow the children to approach or greet the new teacher at their own pace.	❑	❑	❑
Take cues from the children about how much help they need in responding to the change. Don't expect them to be done reacting quickly, since feelings are complicated and can recur. On the other hand, don't overdo it by projecting your own feelings of loss or disruption onto them, for example by asking repeatedly whether they are sad because a particular person left.	❑	❑	❑

Add your own suggestions:

Helping Staff Cope With Turnover

When turnover happens, everyone's job can get harder, and everyone can use more help from each other. The more specific you can be about what you need, the better you'll be able to make a plan that truly "cares for the caregivers" during times of transition.

	We currently do this	This is a priority to work on	Not a priority at this time
➡ COMMUNICATING ABOUT A TURNOVER EVENT			
Maintain an atmosphere of open communication and support between administrator and staff when turnover happens—preferably, daily check-ins about substitute staffing and the status of the search for a new staff member.	❑	❑	❑
Director/administrator should inform staff as soon as possible about an upcoming change in staffing, keeping in mind a clear confidentiality policy about what types of information can and cannot be shared.	❑	❑	❑
Provide a letter or memo from the director/administrator to the families in the center, in order to prevent the spread of rumors, take any undue burden off other staff in communicating with parents about the change in staffing, and help staff know what to say when parents bring questions or concerns. Even during an event which may need to be kept confidential, put out a memo containing as much information as possible.	❑	❑	❑
Provide a place for staff to discuss the situation and even to "blow off steam" when turnover happens, so that feelings can be expressed and resolved as they emerge, instead of lingering and clouding staff's ability to work together as a team.	❑	❑	❑
Director/administrator should offer support and acknowledgment to staff that they are doing a good job during the hectic and demanding periods when turnover happens. Recognize and reward the "extras" they do, and guard against dumping additional duties on them. (Bring in lunch one day, for example, or hold a teacher recognition event.)	❑	❑	❑
When a staff member has been terminated, the director/administrator should communicate clearly to staff about the reasons for the termination if these can be given. Without such information, others may needlessly fear the loss of their own jobs, and many rumors may circulate.	❑	❑	❑

Helping Staff Cope With Turnover
continued

	We currently do this	This is a priority to work on	Not a priority at this time
Administrators should ask for support from other administrators, and obtain legal advice as necessary, about how to handle turnover situations.	❑	❑	❑

Add your own suggestions:

➡ INTEGRATING NEW PEOPLE

	We currently do this	This is a priority to work on	Not a priority at this time
Arrange for substitutes and others to fill staffing gaps and maintain continuity, preferably people whom the staff, children and parents already know.	❑	❑	❑
Provide a thorough orientation and training period for new staff, and make an investment in staff meeting time and staff development activities for the entire staff.	❑	❑	❑
Allow time for relationship-building among new co-workers, rather than simply thrusting a new situation upon them; for example, giving teaching teams a daily time to meet, plan, and exchange feedback.	❑	❑	❑
Acknowledge, appreciate and reward the extra work of orientation, training and/or mentoring that experienced staff (especially head teachers) take on when new staff join the program.	❑	❑	❑
Arrange for a substitute or "floater" to help out in the classroom when a new person is receiving orientation and/or on-the-job training, so that there is at least one person extra.	❑	❑	❑
Establish a buddy system in which a staff member "adopts" the new person for a certain period (e.g., a month), making herself especially available to meet, talk and answer questions.	❑	❑	❑
Create transition rituals for departing and arriving staff, such as parties, potlucks, personal letters, and "welcome" and "good-bye" signs to decorate the classroom.	❑	❑	❑

Add your own suggestions:

Helping Staff Cope With Turnover
continued

	We currently do this	This is a priority to work on	Not a priority at this time

➡ GENERAL PROGRAM POLICIES

	We currently do this	This is a priority to work on	Not a priority at this time
Develop written personnel policies, as well as clear job descriptions for all staff positions, with input from staff.	❏	❏	❏
Hold regular staff meetings, and create other ongoing opportunities for communication, check-ins and positive feedback between administrator and staff.	❏	❏	❏
Outline and circulate a clear organizational structure and supervisory ladder, so that all staff will have an agreed-on procedure about where (and to whom) to address concerns and questions.	❏	❏	❏
Involve staff in all phases of the program's recruitment and hiring process, from start to finish.	❏	❏	❏
Develop a clear and equitable policy on staff break times, so that this is not something that "falls through the cracks" at times of turnover, when staff may need breaks the most.	❏	❏	❏
Require advance notice of departure whenever possible (at least two weeks, but preferably more), and discuss the policy so that all staff understand the implications of leaving a job abruptly.	❏	❏	❏
Provide regular opportunities for evaluation.	❏	❏	❏
Promote staff professionalism and opportunities for ongoing training, education and advancement.	❏	❏	❏
Arrange for staff development sessions on conflict resolution skills and other turnover-related topics.	❏	❏	❏
Develop a clear policy on confidentiality; i.e., when personnel and other matters can and cannot be discussed publicly.	❏	❏	❏
Assist staff members who may need to leave child care employment in reaching the decision to move on—either through taking a leave of absence, departing voluntarily, or, if necessary, being terminated. Do not allow an inappropriate job placement or hiring decision to "drag out" indefinitely, which creates a burden on other staff.	❏	❏	❏

Add your own suggestions:

Helping Parents Cope with Turnover

When parents are informed in advance about turnover, and helped in forming relationships with new staff, they are likely to feel more comfortable about the transition and better able to help their children adjust.

	We currently do this	This is a priority to work on	Not a priority at this time
Invite parents to spend time in the classroom and see their child's program in action. Parents should always feel welcome to visit.	❑	❑	❑
Inform parents about impending staff changes as far in advance as possible. This could take the form of individual conversations, a parent memo, or a letter from the staff member who will be leaving.	❑	❑	❑
Offer suggestions to parents about ways they can help their child, and/or help in the classroom, during the period of change.	❑	❑	❑
Invite parents to a "farewell" event for the departing teachers.	❑	❑	❑
Include a brief general discussion of staff turnover in your parent handbook, talking about why it's common in the child care field. Alternatively, write an article on the topic for the center newsletter, or a parent memo, at a time when staff turnover is not happening in your center. While this may raise some feelings of anxiety among parents, talking about turnover in context can help make them allies in your broader efforts to manage and prevent it.	❑	❑	❑
Inform parents of your staffing plan for the transition period as soon as you have developed it.	❑	❑	❑
Introduce substitutes to parents. Inform parents whether the substitute will be working on a short-term or long-term basis, and how long she is expected to be in the room.	❑	❑	❑
Involve parents in screening and interviewing job candidates.	❑	❑	❑
Make occasions for parents to meet newly hired staff members—informally at the beginning or end of the day, and perhaps also at a parent meeting or special "welcome" event.	❑	❑	❑

Add your own suggestions:

ACTIVITY

EXIT INTERVIEWS

If you do not do this already, try conducting a brief, informal "exit interview" the next time a staff person plans to leave your center. If a particular departure is a tense one, an exit interview might be less successful. But we often miss these opportunities to understand more clearly why people are leaving and what, if anything, might have made a difference in encouraging them to stay.

1. Ask the staff member which if any of the following were significant factors in the decision to leave, and what changes in the workplace might have made a difference:

➡ pay

➡ benefits

➡ staffing

➡ center personnel policies

➡ the nature of the work itself

➡ relationships with co-workers

➡ opportunities (or lack of opportunities) for professional development

➡ others?

2. Ask what, if anything, the person might suggest adding to the center's turnover reduction plan.

CALCULATING THE RATE OF TURNOVER FOR YOUR PROGRAM

The *job turnover* rate for a child care center—the percentage of teaching staff who leave the center during a given period of time (typically, a year—is measured in the following way:

FORMULA: Divide (a) the number of teaching staff who have left the center, by (b) the number of teaching staff on the center payroll when the program is fully staffed.

For example, if the number of teaching staff who have left in the past year (a) is 6, and the entire number of teaching staff on the center payroll (b) is 20, then the turnover rate is three-tenths, or 30 percent. Turnover rates can also be calculated in this way for each position or classroom in a program. Thus, you can calculate job turnover rates separately for head teachers and assistant teachers, for different classrooms within a center, or for different sites within a multi-site agency.

Formal surveys of child care turnover within a given community, often conducted as part of a salaries and benefits survey, rely on the accuracy of the people supplying the information—typically, center directors. For jobs that turn over most frequently, such as aides or assistant teachers, directors often find it difficult to retain precise information, and often underestimate the actual turnover rate. This method of calculating turnover also fails to capture position turnover (e.g. an assistant becoming a teacher, or a teacher moving to a new site or classroom) within a center or program.

A *staff census* can be a more reliable way to calculate job turnover, and it also provides a means of capturing *position turnover*. The director (or other designated person) lists the name of each staff person and her/his classroom assignment. At a second point in time—one year later, for example—the director indicates which people are still employed, whether their classroom assignments have changed, and the names of any employees hired since the prior data collection point, including those who may have stayed only briefly. This information is then analyzed to determine turnover rates. A census can also include information about salaries, lengths of tenure, and professional backgrounds for each employee, resulting in a detailed picture not only of how many but also which staff are staying or leaving—for example, the more or less trained, or the better or worse paid, among the teachers. This method, however, requires a significant investment of time from the census-taker, as well as a longer wait to learn results.

Data on *occupational turnover* are difficult to collect because there is seldom a way to contact people once they have left a job, in order to learn whether they have remained working in child care or not. When teaching staff are surveyed directly, however, or when a program collects census data as described above, and staff provide personal contact information about themselves, a follow-up survey can be conducted to determine their present occupations.

In the National Child Care Staffing Study first conducted in 1988, for example, the Center for the Child Care Workforce contacted all 1,300 teachers in the study six months after they were first surveyed, and we were able to determine not only how many had left their jobs but how many continued to work in child care. Because few training programs or employers collect ongoing data about their students or employees, however, most information about occupational turnover in child care is anecdotal and imprecise. The federal government collects separation data by industry in order to project training needs for different occupations, using the Current Population Survey. The government tracks people who change their occupational codes between one data collection period and another. However, because the government classifies people working in child care in overlapping categories, these data are also imprecise and provide little direct information about stability within the field (CCW, 1998b).

CALCULATING THE COST OF TURNOVER

What are the direct and indirect expenses incurred by a child care center when a teacher leaves, and how can programs recognize these costs? Because so many costs associated with turnover involve assessing largely invisible expenditures related to how people spend their time, calculations will generally be educated estimates at best.

We know, for example, that when a

SAMPLE STAFF CENSUS

TIME 1	NAME	EDUCATION/ TRAINING	SALARY PER HOUR	START DATE	CURRENT POSITION	END DATE
1/98	J. Doe	CDA	$8.25	1/97	Aide, Rm A	—
1/98	S. Smith	BA	$10.50	3/95	Head Teacher, Rm A	4/98
1/98	F. Jackson	12 units	$ 6.25	9/97	Aide, Rm B	2/98
1/98	L. Stein	CDA	$8.50	1/96	Teacher, Rm B	—

TIME 2	NAME	EDUCATION/ TRAINING	SALARY PER HOUR	START DATE	CURRENT POSITION	END DATE
1/99	J. Doe	CDA	$9.00	1/97	Teacher, Rm A	—
1/99	L. Stein	CDA	$9.50	1/96	Teacher, Rm B	—
1/99	D. Garcia	BA	$11.50	6/98	Head Teacher, Rm A	—
1/99	G. Bruce	12 units	$6.75	2/98	Aide, Rm B	3/98
1/99	L. Well	12 units	$7.50	3/98	Aide, Rm B	—

co-worker leaves, this not only creates more work for those who are left behind, but often affects the energy and focus that people bring to their jobs, at least for a while. In most industries, less than a quarter of turnover costs are spent directly on such items as advertising, hiring substitutes and replacements; most costs involve staff time. Some staff time may be easy to calculate, such as the time spent interviewing job candidates, but other activities, such as the time spent integrating a new person into a classroom team, are harder to assess.

Turnover costs will vary considerably across programs, reflecting differences in rates of pay. The nature and timing of the event will also affect costs. At the beginning of a new year, when children shift to new classrooms, for example, a teacher can be integrated relatively easily if she is well trained. Mid-year is a more difficult time, when relationships and rhythms have been established among children, parents and co-workers. A tense termination my involve legal, mediation or consulting services, which are not necessary when someone leaves under more positive circumstances.

Despite these difficulties, however, many industries and employers struggle through the calculations because the cost estimate helps them to see how their resources are being used and to identify areas for change. Depending on the skill and wage level of an employee, turnover costs can run from several hundred dollars per employee

to as high as 1.5 times an employee's annual salary. These calculations are based on some variation of a basic model which looks at direct and indirect costs incurred during the ***separation or departure process*** (when an employee decides to leave, and actually does so), the ***recruitment and hiring phase***, and the ***post-employment phase*** (the training and orientation process, which usually extends for at least a year, until the employee is fully integrated into the position).

As one teacher in San Mateo, California, observed: "You spend lots of time building personal relationships. Even if I have been in on the hiring, I don't know where the new teacher is coming from until we begin to work together. I feel 'thrown in' with new people. There's not enough orientation or training at my center, so we need to do lots of communication and ask lots of questions. That means other things don't get done, or at least not during paid time. Especially when there are subs prior to a permanent hire, I give up lunch hours, and I stay late to greet all of the parents and to reassure them if we had a difficult day, at least at first. The children get more stressed and there's more conflict, so a lot of my time is spent 'putting out fires.' I can't do as much creative intervention to head off conflict before it begins."

Many of the indirect costs are challenging to calculate because they involve assessing the lost productivity not only of the departing or new employee, but also of the employees who work closely with them. Costs of turnover are generally assumed to be higher in such workplaces as child care centers, where team work is essential to effectiveness. In many other industries, lost productivity is easy to calculate in terms of fewer products made or fewer clients served. In child care, productivity relates to enrollment and to quality of service. Turnover may affect enrollment, either because families leave in response to it, or because a program cannot enroll to its full capacity due to staff shortages. But lost productivity in terms of a decline in the quality of services— although it is a very real phenomenon, as described above—is difficult to translate into monetary terms.

Through our work with directors and teaching staff, we have grappled with these issues and developed instruments (found on pages 65-68) to assess the cost of turnover in child care programs. Initially, we asked people to brainstorm the different types of expenses incurred when turnover occurs. We asked training participants to distinguish between direct and indirect costs. We also asked them to list in detail the missed opportunities—i.e., things that didn't get done—because turnover happened. From these discussions, we drafted log forms and asked teachers and administrators to use them, either to keep track of expenditures and missed opportunities for a set period of time, or to track

Turnover costs can run from several hundred dollars per employee to as high as 1.5 times an employee's annual salary.

costs around a specific turnover event. Most chose to follow the latter approach. We also asked directors and teachers which type of information-gathering worked best for them: being interviewed, keeping track of costs on a tape recorder, or filling out a form. Most chose to use the written form included here.

We tried to create as simple a method as possible for tracking turnover costs. Many industries use highly mathematical formulas for tracking and calculating turnover costs, especially those that are associated with employees reaching an expected level of proficiency in their jobs (Creery, 1986; Dawson, 1988; Phillips, 1990; Rousseau, 1984). Weighing the many demands on child care personnel, we chose to present an easier and less precise method of tracking and calculating turnover, but one which can generate sufficient information for the purposes of education, advocacy and planning in most programs.

KEEPING A LOG TO MEASURE THE COSTS OF TURNOVER

When turnover takes place, you can use the following log forms to measure the many costs involved. The form for directors primarily lists many of the administrative functions associated with finding and replacing staff, and

SAMPLE COSTS OF
TEACHER TURNOVER AT ONE CENTER

Period of time: One month

Description of Event: Teacher leaving, one week notice

Direct Costs: $2,144.50 (primarily substitutes and advertising)

Indirect Costs:* 21.75 hours of director time @ $18.50 per hour including benefits (meetings with staff, writing parent letter, writing ad, screening, interviews, subbing in classroom); 13.25 hours of teacher time @ $14.00 per hour including benefits (meeting, interviews, talking with parents).

Period of time: One month

Description of Event: Teaching assistant promoted, new assistant hired

Direct Costs: $322.75

Indirect Costs: 12.75 hours of director time @ $18.50 per hour including benefits (meetings with staff, writing parent letter, writing ad, screening, interviews, subbing in classroom); 9 hours of teacher time @ $14.00 per hour including benefits (meetings, interviews, talking with parents).

Missed Opportunities: Canceled staff in-service training, missed director support group, delayed re-write of brochure. ★

*Staff time is calculated as an indirect cost, because cost would be incurred regardless of turnover. If overtime is paid, it would be a direct cost.

the teacher form captures classroom activities related to turnover. Each form, however, provides space to capture both types of expenditures. The head teacher in each classroom should receive a new form for each week you are tracking costs. You may choose to fill them out for a month or even longer, but remember that the longer you keep the log, the greater the job of compiling the results will be. Once staff time spent on turnover is tallied, costs can be assigned by multiplying

staff hours by specific rates of pay (see sample above).

It is important to distinguish between direct and indirect staff costs, as the latter usually represent already budgeted costs. Indirect costs, which are surprisingly high in most occupations, capture and underscore how wasteful and draining turnover is.

The tallied information can be useful in budgeting, planning, and advocacy efforts, because it can help you spell out the ways in which turnover consumes time and human resources in your program. Within the center, the turnover logs can help staff understand the issues that the director or administrator is facing, and vice versa. Teachers may feel somewhat less frustrated when they realize the many steps involved in hiring a replacement; and directors may become more attuned to the added pressures that teachers experience when a co-worker leaves.

The information is also useful for communicating with parents and the board of directors or owners about the urgency of the turnover problem. You may also be able to identify how you could save your center money and resources for meeting other needs by reducing your turnover costs. One center in our group was able to convince their hiring committee, comprised of parent and community representatives who were notoriously slow in scheduling and conducting interviews, to move faster, when they realized how substitute costs were mounting with each day of delay.

On a larger scale, as we noted in the Preface, the U.S. Military Child Care system successfully used their calculations of turnover costs as an argument for instituting a caregiver compensation and training plan that has drastically reduced turnover system-wide. And while your center or your community may not be able to reap such benefits so soon, clear information about the costs of turnover can be a great help in figuring out how those funds might be better spent in turnover *prevention*.

MAKING A PLAN TO MANAGE TURNOVER

Child care programs face the challenge of creating an environment in which all staff can freely express their feelings about change, and work together as a team to deal most effectively with it. An atmosphere of shared decision-making among staff can ease the burden that many administrators feel in having to solve turnover problems alone. What's more, an open and democratic process that everyone feels part of will also have a greater chance of succeeding. (For more on "participatory management" and shared decision making, see Part 3, page 76.)

In Part 3, we will discuss ways to develop a turnover *reduction* plan, to keep it from happening so often in the future. The present discussion focuses on making a turnover *management* plan, to help make it less stressful and disruptive whenever it does occur. Such a process might develop in the following way:

1. Acknowledge new information

The director or administrator may announce, for example, "As you may have heard, Jane is leaving in two weeks, and it's very unlikely that we can find a replacement teacher by then. We'll have to figure out some adjustments in our routines and staffing over the next month."

2. Elicit feedback

It's importance to ask for feedback as much as possible with open-ended

Week Beginning _____ - _____ - _____

Person completing form _____

Number of positions changing* _____

*If you wish to track costs by each event or if more than 2 events are occurring at one time, use additional forms.

COST CATEGORY Leave blank if category is not applicable	DIRECT COSTS Report amount of *money* spent by the Center	INDIRECT COSTS Report amount of time *you* spent this week	INDIRECT COSTS* Report amount of time spent by *other* staff this week	MISSED OPPORTUNITIES Record things you could not do because of dealing with turnover-related issues
DEPARTURE				
Interviewing staff about incidents leading to staff departure				
Informing and conferencing with parents, board members, staff, volunteers re: departure				
Re-arranging duties and schedules				
Locating substitute or replacement staff				
Classroom coverage (substitute costs or staff time including director)				
Writing communications for personnel files; other forms or documentation for grievance procedures				
Updating library, attending workshops re: labor laws, unemployment information				
Talking with licensing re: unusual incidents				
Mediation services if needed				
Legal consultation if needed				
Severance package				

*Record non-teaching staff costs here. Indirect costs from teaching staff logs will be incorporated on the final page of this log.

DIRECTOR—COST OF TURNOVER LOG, PAGE 2

COST CATEGORY Leave blank if category is not applicable	DIRECT COSTS Report amount of money spent by the Center	INDIRECT COSTS Report amount of time you spent this week	INDIRECT COSTS* Report amount of time spent by other staff this week	MISSED OPPORTUNITIES Record things you could not do because of dealing with turnover-related issues
Paying out accumulated leave for sick or personal days				
Higher unemployment or worker's comp rates, continuation of medical coverage for separated employee				
Loss of enrollment capacity (can't meet ratios)				
Loss of families (damage to reputation)				
Going away party or gift				
More stress, illness, more substitutes				
Other, please describe				
SUBTOTAL				
RECRUITMENT AND HIRING PHASE				
Advertising (ads, mailing, calls or visits to colleges)				
Screening and interviewing applicants				
Checking references				
Processing fingerprint and TB tests				
Processing new hire payroll, benefits				
Classroom coverage (substitutes or staff time including director)				
Overtime if staff covers for separated employee				
Arranging for substitutes to cover staff participation in hiring interviews				

*Record non-teaching staff costs here. Indirect costs from teaching staff logs will be incorporated on the final page of this log.

DIRECTOR—COST OF TURNOVER LOG, PAGE 3

COST CATEGORY Leave blank if category is not applicable	DIRECT COSTS Report amount of *money* spent by the Center	INDIRECT COSTS Report amount of time *you* spent this week	INDIRECT COSTS* Report amount of time spent by *other* staff this week	MISSED OPPORTUNITIES Record things you could not do because of dealing with turnover-related issues
Loss of enrollment capacity (can't meet ratios)				
Loss of families (damage to reputation)				
Recruitment of new families				
Double staffing to insure overlap between old and new staff				
Other, please describe				
SUBTOTAL				
POST-EMPLOYMENT PHASE				
Orientation				
Introduction of new employee to agency, parents, and children				
Training				
Set up (assigning cubby, voice mail, personnel policies)				
New classroom materials				
Parent meetings and conferences				
Classroom observation				
Other, please describe				
SUBTOTAL				
SUBTOTAL: Departure, Recruitment/ Hiring and Post-Employment Phases				
SUBTOTAL: Indirect Teaching Staff Costs (from Teacher Logs)				
TOTAL: ALL COSTS				

*Record non-teaching staff costs here. Indirect costs from teaching staff logs will be incorporated at the bottom of the page.

TEACHER—COST OF TURNOVER LOG

Week Beginning ___-___-___

Person completing form _____ Title _____

Number of positions changing* _____

*If you wish to track costs by each event or if more than 2 events are occurring at one time, use additional forms.

COST CATEGORY Leave blank if category is not applicable	AMOUNT OF TIME YOU SPENT THIS WEEK	AMOUNT OF TIME SPENT BY OTHER STAFF IN YOUR CLASSROOM THIS WEEK**	MISSED OPPORTUNITIES Record things you could not do because of dealing with turnover-related issues
BEFORE/DURING THE DEPARTURE			
Meeting or discussions with director, other staff, parents			
Planning how to prepare children for the departure			
Rearranging duties and coverage			
Planning, attending farewell party			
HIRING AND BEYOND			
Screening and interviewing applicants			
Orienting new employee			
Training new person			
Meetings with parents, co-workers, directors			
Buying new equipment			
THROUGHOUT PROCESS			
Calling substitutes			
More stress, more illness, more absences			
Other, please describe			
TOTAL			

** If there is more than one staff member for whom you are recording time, place each person's initials next to the amount of time they spent, to assist whomever makes the final calculations.

questions, rather than "closed" questions that seem to expect a certain kind of answer. For example: "What are your concerns about Jane's leaving? How will you and your classroom be affected by her leaving? What is your biggest fear about this change?" Allow for and acknowledge negative feelings, critical input, doubts and difficulties. Listen without reacting immediately, and perhaps use chart paper to list everyone's responses and concerns. It may be natural for a director (or other bearer of the news) to feel that it is her fault and to personalize these reactions. Instead, try to remain open to what people are saying, and especially avoid countering negative comments right away with a positive. The group may need to get their full say before they can move toward solutions and plans of action.

If there is little or no response at first, it may mean that people are unsure about whether it's safe to express feelings and opinions in a staff meeting. They may be more accustomed to talking among themselves elsewhere, such as in the staff room or out in the parking lot. To elicit more responses, and to show your openness to whatever may come up, some humor may be useful, or asking more open-ended questions, or expressing some of your own doubts or negative feelings. You may also need to return to the topic again later, opening up the dialogue repeatedly until people feel more comfortable.

3. Clear up any misconceptions or rumors

Ask, for example, "Do you have any questions about the reasons why Jane is leaving?" In the case of a termination, a director may not be able to give much information because of an employee's legal right to confidentiality, but it may be possible to dispel rumors, and to review the program's policies on the grounds for termination. (These, along with a statement on confidentiality, should already be available in writing in a program handbook.) If anyone probes for information that cannot be divulged, it may be necessary to ask whether there are any underlying concerns: for example, are they uncertain about the center's policies, or afraid of losing their own jobs? Try and address these concerns rather than focusing on the details of the present situation.

4. Brainstorm a plan

Ask for suggestions and ideas on how to make the change as smooth as possible: "How can we adjust the schedule or the staffing to cope with this change, and minimize the impact on children, parents and staff?" As a group, you can also use the checklists for children, staff and parents included in this chapter.

5. Discuss broader solutions

If time permits, talk about what the staff as a whole can do together to make these transitions easier in the future. Or even better, set up a staff

ACTIVITY

DEVELOPING A TURNOVER MANAGEMENT PLAN

Using the checklists beginning on page 51, develop a plan for your program that addresses children's needs for continuity, staff's needs for communication and clarity, parents' needs for information and reassurance, and the director's needs for staff teamwork and support for center policies.

Ideally, each staff member will answer these questions individually. Then, all staff will meet to discuss their responses and their areas of agreement and disagreement, and based on these, will develop a turnover management plan together.

✓ Describe at least two changes your program will make to improve how turnover is handled when it occurs. The changes can involve practices with children, parents or staff.

1.

2.

3.

✓ In each case, describe how the particular situation was handled previously, and why the change is an improvement from current practice.

1.

2.

3.

✓ Describe what barriers, if any, are in the way of change, and what role you might play in helping to overcome them.

1.

2.

3.

Some examples: A surprising number of programs that have participated in our Taking On Turnover trainings have said that they never formally inform parents when a staff member is leaving; in effect, parents would "just notice eventually," and the word would spread. Just as surprisingly, a number of programs noted that they do not formally notify the staff about such staffing changes, either—for example, the date of departure, the plans for substitute and replacement staff, the timing of the transition and hiring process, etc. Many of these programs have now decided to institute regular, more formalized processes for sharing turnover information with parents and staff in the future.

In other instances, child care programs have made plans to:

➡ create a "welcome" sign for all new staff, with a picture of that person

➡ hold a staff in-service training session on talking with children about change

➡ create a one-week overlap between departing and newly arriving staff members whenever possible ("well worth the cost," as staff in one program observed)

➡ conduct exit interviews with departing staff members, to learn more about the issues behind turnover in their programs

➡ conduct farewell and welcome circles—not only for children, but for staff.

meeting or in-service training event solely devoted to this topic—again, using the checklists as a guide. Keep a chart or other record of all suggestions, and share them in your newsletter.

6. Ask for support and commitment

At the end of the discussion, as a way to summarize and reinforce the decisions you've reached, the discussion leader might say, "It seems clear that we need to change the morning schedules to cover Jane's shift when she leaves. Can I count on your support in making this change?" Naturally, this will be more likely if staff have been involved in the planning process and have a sense of "ownership" in any decisions that have been reached.

7. Follow through

Keep a record of the process by checking in regularly with individual staff and as a group, to offer and receive feedback on how the transition plan is working. This might need to be a relatively formal and systematic evaluation process if the program is consid-ering longer-term changes in staffing, scheduling or other arrangements. It may then be necessary to modify the work plan if it doesn't realistically fit current abilities and resources. Above all, staff need to receive acknowledgment and appreciation for their hard work and extra effort during this time of change.

▪ ▪ ▪

Periods of turnover can be times of stress, tension and overwork. But the more consciously the program works at managing turnover when it occurs, they can also be times of team-building and constructive change—and they may point the way toward things you can do to prevent turnover from happening so often.

In the next section of this book, we will move from turnover management plans to turnover reduction plans: concrete ways to examine work environments, hiring practices, compensation, and substitute policies in your program in order to reduce turnover in the future.

Part 3
MAKING AN ACTION PLAN TO REDUCE TURNOVER IN YOUR PROGRAM

Most industries try to stabilize their workforce by focusing on improving the work environment, hiring practices and compensation. These "big three" issues encompass the reasons why most people decide whether or not to remain at their jobs.

In the following pages, we provide a framework for exploring the three central issues of work environments, hiring and compensation in child care centers, and we have added a section on recruiting, hiring and retaining substitutes. Each section contains activities for tackling these questions pro-actively, and exploring what may be holding your program back from making progress. At the end of Part 3, we then discuss how to put the pieces together to make a "turnover reduction plan" for your program.

DIFFERENT JOB ROLES, SIMILAR DESIRES

We have consistently found in our training sessions that teachers and directors express very similar desires about changes in the workplace they would most like to make in order to reduce turnover. Although they may have different emphases or priorities, teaching staff and administrators do not necessarily define a good work environment very differently from each other, and depending on how the program is structured, they do not necessarily have conflicting interests.

During a training series for teaching staff and administrators from 20 San Francisco Bay Area centers, we tallied the top three workplace items that each group said would reduce turnover the most. Teaching staff rated "better pay and benefits" as the top priority; "a better substitute system" ranked second; and three items, "more staff," "more preparation time" and "more scheduled break time," ranked third. Likewise, directors identified "better pay and benefits" as the top priority, and two items tied for second place: "a better substitute system" and "more staff."

Other desires most frequently mentioned by teachers included:

- public recognition and understanding of child care work;

- more staff education and training paid for by the center;

- equitable treatment;

- better communication;

- more meeting and planning time;

- better parent-teacher communication;

- more appreciation and respect for staff;

- better-trained staff;

- better orientation of new staff; and

- better playgrounds.

Other desires among directors included:

- a better hiring process;

- better staff morale and commitment to the field;

- staff with higher qualifications;

- more staff development paid for by the center;

- more meeting and planning time for staff;

- a staff lounge;

- better communication; and

- a director support group. ★

1

SECTION 1. YOUR PROGRAM'S WORK ENVIRONMENT

"Work environment" is a broad term that encompasses many aspects of what it is like to work in a particular setting. It includes the interpersonal climate of a workplace, such as your relationships with co-workers, the ways in which decisions are made, the lines of communication, and patterns of power and leadership among staff. It also includes the policies and practices that define employees' working conditions, such as vacation and sick leave, job descriptions, grievance procedures, and provisions to ensure workers' health and safety.

Taking on turnover requires close attention to all these aspects of a work environment— beginning with the ways in which staff members work together and relate to each other.

> The quality of working relationships in a child care program strongly affects whether staff will decide to stay on the job or leave.

WORK RELATIONSHIPS

In the child care field, our training generally prepares us to understand and promote healthy child development, and to foster positive, nurturing relationships with and among children. By contrast, we tend to spend very little time working on the issues of adult development, and how to build good working and learning relationships among adults. Since child care involves so many adult-to-adult interactions, this is a serious gap in our preparation. A quality child care program maintains strong relationships with parents and the wider community; and it establishes a positive work environment where effective supervision, mentoring and teamwork take place among co-workers. But too often, our lack of attention to adult issues hampers our ability to create such an environment.

The quality of working relationships in a child care program strongly affects whether staff will decide to stay on the job or leave. Our relationships with co-workers are the product of several interrelated concerns:

➡ the management style of administrators and other leaders in the program;

➡ power: who has it and does not have it, and to what extent it is shared;

➡ issues of race, class and culture: the degree to which all voices and perspectives are heard and honored; and

➡ professional respect between managers and staff, among staff, and between staff and parents.

Like all organizations, child care programs are "social systems." Individuals in a social system need to feel that they are a valuable and respected part of the whole, so that they can share a natural sense of "ownership" of and commitment to the center's health and well-being. Each adult needs to feel able to contribute his or her knowledge and perspectives, just as we want every child to feel valued and involved in making decisions that affect their daily lives. But as a profession, we are often more democratic and participatory in spirit with children than we are among ourselves.

Power relationships and conflicts among adults are especially challenging. In such a "giving" profession as child care, many of us are wary of conflict and even try to wish it away. Although we may be superb at helping children cope with conflict, we often don't acknowledge strains between co-workers or between staff and management. We don't always clearly recognize the power relationships—official or unofficial, written or unwritten—that exist in any workplace. On the contrary, it's not uncommon to hear adults in child care programs say, "We get along just like a family," or "We're all so close," or "I don't really have any power here as a director. No one thinks of me as 'the boss.'" But closer examination may reveal that only some people in the program feel safe to express themselves directly to one another or share their opinions.

If you are a teacher, do you feel that your input is asked for when important decisions come up, and does it feel safe to give it? Or do you feel that some people's suggestions are heard and others are ignored? Is there an atmosphere of openness and listening? Do decision-making processes focus on the issues involved, rather than the personalities?

If you are an administrator, do you find that staff sometimes (or often) talk to each other about problems and concerns, but not to you? Does the real staff meeting take place afterward, in the teachers' lounge or out in the parking lot? If you direct an agency that has more than one work site, do you feel isolated or "at arm's length" from staff? If you work in a middle management position, do you indeed feel caught in the middle when conflicts arise?

This chapter is designed to help you explore these questions as they relate to your workplace, and to reflect on how they may be affecting staff turnover in your program and your ability to do something about it.

> In child care, we tend to spend very little time on the issues of adult development. We are often more democratic and participatory in spirit with children than we are among ourselves.

PARTICIPATORY MANAGEMENT

Before you can truly make an action plan to reduce turnover, it's important to grapple with how your program currently does other kinds of planning, problem solving and decision making. To what extent are these processes the exclusive domain of one or several people, and to what extent are they shared?

The terms "participatory management," "shared participation" and "shared decision making" refer to a work environment in which the administration and the teaching staff work together to develop and operate the program. Shared participation can be promoted in a variety of ways—for example, through:

➡ staff meetings in which all staff have input into the agenda;

➡ training sessions on problem-solving and team work;

➡ staff/supervisor conferences;

➡ problem solving teams that are empowered to research ideas and solutions, and to come back and present results or proposals to the entire staff;

➡ collective bargaining between unionized staff members and the management of a child care program.

When all staff share in the decision-making process, they have a greater commitment to achieving the program's goals and objectives, and the quality of the child care they provide is enhanced because they are involved in shaping it. Shared decision making involves getting all stakeholders together and allowing each person's opinions, ideas and vote to carry equal weight in solving problems. Leadership, in this model, is based on the idea that the person with the best skills, knowl-

edge, interest and energy for a particular issue should take leadership on it.

Perhaps your program is more accustomed to a top-down management style, in which administrators make all major decisions and the other staff carry them out. But although the idea of "participatory management" may sound far-fetched or antithetical to you, child care programs have found it to be of enormous benefit to teaching staff and administrators alike. Teachers come to feel more trusted, resourceful and capable as they help shape the work environment. And just as importantly, managers begin to feel less isolated and overburdened—less like the proverbial "Mom" who is expected to be in charge of everything, the one who constantly bears bad news and takes the flak whenever tough decisions must be made.

But shared decision making doesn't just come naturally. Many people are not accustomed to a work environment where what they say really matters or is listened to. It may take staff awhile to trust that it's "for real" when a child care program begins moving in this direction. They may need help in building the skills and confidence necessary for speaking up, analyzing and solving problems, and participating in shaping programs and policies. Otherwise, the few staff members who are more comfortable with such an approach may tend to dominate all the meetings and decision making processes, in which case you have simply replaced one form of hierarchy with another. Moving to a participatory management style is a learning and training process in itself, and needs to be recognized as such. It is essential to be clear from the start, too, about any limits to the staff's decision making influence—for example, restrictions imposed by licensing regulations—so that they don't feel deceived afterward, or feel that the process was not so open after all.

The following case example outlines a process for participatory management and teamwork.

Identifying the problem

Let's say that two teachers in a child care program have talked with each other and feel that the staff do not receive enough paid sick days. In a participatory environment, all staff would feel welcome to bring such issues to the staff as a whole, rather than feeling excluded from making decisions about them. And by the same token, all would feel responsible for taking issues through the proper group channels, rather than harboring resentments, sowing divisiveness or spreading rumors.

Gathering information

The staff members who have identified this issue prepare to present it to the group, including all available current information. This may mean that they will need to do some research and information gathering to put a presen-

> **In a participatory environment, teachers feel more trusted and capable, and managers feel less isolated and overburdened.**

tation together—for example, finding out the amount of sick leave that other local programs offer, or checking to see what is recommended in the CCW publication, *Creating Better Child Care Jobs: Model Work Standards for Teaching Staff in Center-Based Child Care* (CCW, 1998a). (We will return to a discussion of the Model Work Standards later in this chapter, on page 89).

Communicating

The two staff members contact the group about the need to discuss the issue—either asking to put it on the agenda at a regularly scheduled meeting, or scheduling a separate meeting at another convenient time. In advance, the presenters might send information out to the group so that everyone will be better prepared to discuss it. This could also include working up the cost implications of different approaches. Note that thinking about costs does not have to be solely the administrator's job; other staff members can take responsibility for developing a financially realistic plan.

Analyzing the problem

At the meeting, the group considers the following: What are the issues? Why is this a problem or concern? Does everyone agree that it is a problem worth working on? Who is affected? What will or could happen if nothing is done? What financial costs are involved? What other barriers, if any, need to be addressed? The group must reach a clear, shared understanding of the problem before it can function in making decisions to solve it.

Brainstorming possible solutions

Someone other than the presenters should act as a facilitator or moderator, as group members put forth their ideas. At this point, nothing should be ruled out; ideas should be allowed to flow freely and creatively, without interrupting, judging or criticizing. Another person should take notes or use chart paper to list these responses. Examples:

✓ One or two additional sick days per year for all staff.

✓ But that would cost x, which we can't afford.

✓ We can make this a priority for our fundraising this year.

✓ We can consider a tuition increase.

✓ We could transfer funds from another item in the budget.

✓ Can people who have accumulated unused sick time donate it to other staff in need? Etc.

Decision making

Next, the group evaluates the merits and drawbacks of each solution, and reaches a decision. Ideally, everyone participates in this discussion and contributes his/her point of view. (See the accompanying article on Decision Making, page 80.)

Developing a plan of action

The group reaches the following decision, to be presented to the Board of Directors at its meeting next month: one additional sick day per year, with a budgetary plan to cover the additional costs, and the commitment to change the policy to two additional sick days in the next budget year. Now, turning this decision into an action plan means taking into account who will do what, when, where, and how. Two or more people should be assigned to be in charge of implementing the plan (in this case, taking it to the Board), and setting up a system for reporting to the group on progress—making sure that tasks are shared among a sufficient number of people. Before the meeting ends, someone in the group should develop a written description of the action plan, to ensure that everyone understands and agrees with it, and that anyone who was absent can receive a copy.

Follow-through

As part of implementing the plan, the group checks up with each other regularly at staff meetings or other occasions about any progress made, and reviews or restructures the plan as needed. Another important part of follow-through is to communicate this progress and success to parents and others in the community.

APPROACHES TO DECISION MAKING

Individuals are more likely to support a decision in which they have played a part. Although it can be difficult to achieve an agreed-upon decision—often because group members have little experience in other approaches besides a traditional "win-lose" model—it is crucial to realize that avoiding a decision is, in fact, a decision: a choice not to move forward or change the status quo.

Group decisions are sometimes made by individuals or subgroups who push through a decision, relying on the passivity of other participants. This is particularly likely to happen when a group is new or unused to making decisions together, and informal leaders emerge who tend to take charge of the decision-making process. All group members, however, can confront that pattern of decision making by commenting on it whenever it occurs, and questioning whether all opinions are being considered.

Decision making methods include:

➤ **Majority vote:** More than half the group members agree on a single choice. A major drawback is that those who voted against the decision may not feel committed to implementing it.

➤ **Unanimous vote:** All group members agree. Problems may arise because some people who feel the pressure to agree may not really support the decision, and because one person can block the decision by disagreeing.

➤ **Consensus:** Internal discussion and polls take place to find common points of agreement. In the course of trying to reach consensus, group members suggest modifications to the original proposal that may be acceptable to others, resulting in a genuine agreement to implement the revised decision. This method, although time-consuming, is most appropriate when important policy decisions are being made.

Many believe that decisions made by consensus are of higher quality than those arrived at through other methods. Consensus is a collective opinion arrived at by a group whose members have listened carefully to the opinions of others, have communicated openly, and have been able to state their opposition to other members' views and seek alternatives in a constructive manner. When a decision is made by consensus, all members—because they have had the opportunity to influence it—should feel they understand the decision and can support it.

Johnson and Johnson (1975) suggest the following guidelines for reaching decisions by consensus:

➡ Avoid blindly arguing for your own individual judgments. Present your position as clearly and logically as possible, but listen to other members' reactions and consider them carefully before you press your point.

➡ Avoid changing your mind only to reach agreement and avoid conflict. Support only solutions to which you are at least somewhat agreeable. Yield only to positions that have an objective and logically sound foundation.

➡ Avoid "conflict-reducing" procedures such as majority vote, tossing a coin, averaging or bargaining in reaching decisions.

➡ Seek out differences of opinion; they are natural and should be expected. Try to involve everyone in the decision process. Disagreements can help the group's decision because they present a wide range of information and opinions, thereby creating a better chance for the group to hit upon more adequate solutions.

➡ Do not assume that someone must win and someone must lose when discussion reaches a stalemate. Instead, look for the next most acceptable alternative for all members.

➡ Discuss underlying assumptions, listen carefully to one another, and encourage the participation of all members. ★

ASSESSING YOUR ORGANIZATION'S WORK CLIMATE

Thanks to the work of Paula Jorde Bloom and her colleagues at the Center for Early Childhood Leadership, a number of tools are available to help you assess your child care program's work climate. Here we include a survey that is recommended for programs with a relatively high level of trust among staff. You might want to use it to clarify your own thinking about your work environment, as well as to share your responses with other staff members.

ACTIVITY

THE WORK CLIMATE

The administrator(s) and teaching staff should all complete this worksheet, then meet to compare responses and note areas of agreement and disagreement; this discussion can provide a springboard for fine tuning how you and your co-workers communicate. If there is a high level of divisiveness among staff, however, or you sense that some staff members may have "hidden agendas," a more formal and anonymous approach to assessing the work climate may be advisable.* For each question, consider:

➡ what works in your present system, and

➡ what needs to be improved.

1. To determine how well your center encourages collegiality among teaching staff:

List the opportunities provided for staff to:

✓ work collaboratively on projects

✓ share resources

✓ solve problems together

* The Center for Early Childhood Leadership will provide survey forms and tally responses from individual staff members and develop a child care program profile for a reasonable fee. (For more information, contact: The Center for Early Childhood Leadership, National-Louis University, 1000 Capitol Drive, Wheeling, Illinois 60090-7201; 708-465-0575, ext. 5551 or 5562.)

2. To determine what opportunities the center provides for professional development:

Describe the opportunities that teaching staff have to:

✓ improve their skills and gain new skills

✓ gain a better understanding of the theories and principles of child development and early childhood education

✓ learn best practices for working with young children

✓ learn strategies that support positive relationships among staff, between staff and children, and between staff and parents

3. What types of feedback do teaching staff members receive about their job performance?

4. How well are job roles and responsibilities defined? How are they explained to staff? How are different roles and responsibilities distinguished?

5. How fair and equitable is the program's reward system? What rewards are available to staff, and how are they administered?

6. To determine how involved staff are in making decisions on important issues:

Identify the types of decisions that teaching staff are empowered to make through a group process.

Identify the types of decisions for which teaching staff's opinions are solicited, and in which their perspectives have an influence. In what ways are opinions obtained from teaching staff?

7. How are teaching staff involved in setting program goals and objectives?

8. How realistic are teaching staff work loads?

9. How conducive is the physical setting to good job performance?

10. How are creativity and innovation encouraged?

(Adapted with author's permission from Bloom, 1997.)

RESPECT FOR DIVERSITY IN CHILD CARE SETTINGS

Inevitably, the quality of your program's work environment involves issues of race, class and culture: for example, whether the composition of the staff reflects the diversity of the families and community you serve, and whether the program has a climate of mutual respect, fairness, understanding and trust. As you work together to "take on turnover," you may find that such issues play out in terms of why different staff members leave, and the priorities for change that different staff members identify.

Teachers who are single parents, for instance, may need better family health coverage or other benefits; perhaps this is even why several of them have left the job in recent years. But others who already have decent benefits through a spouse or partner, or have the means to pay for them, may want better professional development opportunities instead, so that they can complete an advanced degree. Perhaps a local workshop series on "improving your hiring practices" is available, but it's run entirely by European-American trainers who haven't thought about how to recruit teachers from communities of color. Perhaps training events tend to be accessible only to people who own cars. Perhaps whenever a head teacher leaves the center, the women of color in assistant teacher positions consistently feel left out of consideration for the job.

In these and other cases, is everyone in the program really on the same wave-length when it comes to tackling the causes and effects of turnover? Or do "cliques" form among staff along racial or cultural lines, and if so, how are these related to power relationships, who's in the "information loop" or not, who "fits in" with the group as a whole or doesn't, and so on? How does the program seek to bridge differences among the staff, and create equal access to professional development, promotions, decision-making and other opportunities?

Just as we seek to develop culturally diverse and responsive programs for children, we must also be active in promoting open communication, understanding, fairness and respect in working relationships *among adults*. For all of us, becoming fully aware of diversity and committed to challenging prejudice is an ongoing process of learning and practice, and each person is at a different place along the journey. Some people "internalize" the dominant culture's prejudices and stereotypes about their own group to the point where they appear to accept or agree with them. Others may deny differences altogether—saying, for example, that "We're 'color blind' in this program; we see all people as the same," or again, "We get along just like a family."

Whatever the current work environment in your program may be, respect for diversity can't be taken for granted—it takes conscious, dedicated, continuing effort. Louise Derman-Sparks, a

OUR ORIGINS

1. At a staff meeting or retreat, divide into pairs. Each pair then takes turns reflecting on their own family and cultural backgrounds. For example, choose among the following questions. (NOTE: Since this is a long list of suggestions, you don't have to "take on" all of them to have a successful activity!)

- Where were you born? Where did you grow up?

- How would you describe the neighborhood where you were raised?

- What is your ethnic, racial and class heritage?

- What languages or dialects were spoken in your home?

- Did both of your parents work? What were your family's attitudes about work? At what age did you start working?

- Was religion important during your upbringing? If yes, how? If not, what was the most important source of your ethical values?

- Who makes up your family (either your family of origin, or the one you live with now)?

- What traditions does your family follow?

- How do the members of your family relate to each other? For example, how are love, anger, closeness and individuality expressed?

- How is your culture expressed in your family?

- What things are most important for people to know about your racial, ethnic and class identity? What things would you not want people to say about your identity?

2. Reconvene as a large group to discuss these dialogues:

- What did participants learn about each other?

- What was most interesting, important, surprising, challenging?

- Where and how do you see these issues being played out in the workplace?

- Do these issues relate to your program's efforts to tackle staff turnover, and if so, how?

- How might you keep such conversations going in the workplace?

3. As an alternative or follow-up activity: Write in a journal about any of the above topics, or more than one in combination. Then, at a staff meeting or retreat, divide into pairs to discuss what you have written, and then gather as a group to discuss these dialogues.

ACTIVITY

ISSUES OF DIVERSITY IN THE WORKPLACE

This version of the previous activity is geared to identifying specific issues of diversity and inclusiveness in your program. Since this kind of conversation depends on a significant level of openness and trust in the workplace, it may be helpful to have an impartial outside facilitator or trainer assist you. Again, since the activity contains a long list of suggested questions, it is by no means necessary to address all of them at one session.

1. At a staff meeting or retreat, divide into pairs. Each pair then takes turns reflecting on issues of diversity in the workplace. For example, choose among the following questions:

- What values did you learn as a child that you carry into the workplace?

- What did you learn about relationships between children and adults? How were children expected to show respect to adults? How does this influence how you show respect to authority figures or supervisors? How do you know when you are respected by others?

- How are problems solved in your family (either your family of origin or the one you live with now)? How does this influence how you expect problems to be solved in your workplace?

- How does the race or culture of the director/administrator affect the culture of the workplace (for example, in styles of communication, meetings, workplace celebrations, etc.)?

- Have you worked in a place where the director/administrator was of the same race or culture as yourself? How was that different from working with a director/administrator of a different race or culture?

- If you are not a member of the majority racial or cultural group in your program, in what ways have you needed to adapt to different ways of doing things? How did you figure out the "rules" of the dominant group in the program?

- How does your program demonstrate inclusiveness and respect for diversity? In what ways could or should the present climate be improved?

2. Reconvene as a large group to discuss these dialogues:

■ What did participants learn about each other?

■ What was most interesting, important, surprising, challenging?

■ Do these issues relate to your program's efforts to tackle staff turnover, and if so, how?

■ How might you keep such conversations going in the workplace?

3. As an alternative or follow-up activity: Write in a journal about any of the above topics, or more than one in combination. Then, at a staff meeting or retreat, divide into pairs to discuss what you have written, and then gather as a group to discuss these dialogues.

noted anti-bias educator, has written about the stages which adults go through in the effort to unlearn bias and honor diversity (Derman-Sparks, 1989):

➡ **Stage 1: Awareness**—Learning about the patterns and sources of discrimination prevalent in our society, our culture and ourselves. We come to recognize that we have all been scarred by it.

➡ **Stage 2: Exploration**—Digging deeper into the root causes of prejudice; examining our own experiences and origins, and any stereotypes we may have been taught about race, class, ethnicity, sex roles and sexual preference; searching for evidence of bias in our classroom or home learning environments.

➡ **Stage 3: Inquiry**—Asking for more information about causes, roots and symptoms of bias, and seeking out ways of changing those negative patterns and belief systems.

➡ **Stage 4: Reflection**—Sharing with each other what we have learned, what we would like to change, and how we might go about doing so.

➡ **Stage 5: Utilization**—Putting into practice new approaches toward becoming freer from bias: for example, changing one's classroom/home environment, curriculum content, and interactions with others in order to be culturally relevant and respectful of diversity.

These stages can provide you with a framework for embarking and continuing on your own journey, beginning with yourself.

MODEL WORK STANDARDS FOR CHILD CARE PROGRAMS

As a companion volume for your "taking on turnover" activities, we strongly recommend that your program use the Center for the Child Care Workforce publication, *Creating Better Child Care Jobs: Model Work Standards for Teaching Staff in Center-Based Child Care* (CCW, 1998a).

The Model Work Standards set guidelines for all aspects of child care working conditions, organized into 13 categories: wages, benefits, job descriptions, hiring and promotions, grievance procedures, classroom assignments, communication, decision-making and problem-solving, professional development, professional support, diversity, health and safety, and the physical setting. They also offer guidance on how to work as a team to implement them in your center, and how to work with others to implement them more widely in your community.

But although the Model Work Standards are comprehensive in scope, it doesn't mean that you can or should take them all on at once. On the contrary, each child care program can ideally use them to work through a process of identifying one to three top priorities at a time, and making incremental, short-term progress toward long-term goals.

To develop these standards, CCW and the Worthy Wage Campaign conducted a year-long process of building consensus among child care teachers and center directors through a national postcard campaign, focus groups, workshops and other activities, seeking to answer two key questions:

✓ What is a high-quality work environment? and

✓ What needs to be changed to improve your job and your capacity to be a good teacher?

The standards are based on this extensive feedback from the field, combined with research findings on best practices, and they will continue to be refined and adapted as child care programs and communities around the country seek to implement them.

Improving a work environment takes an investment of time, energy and money. Some improvements may require only a minimal financial cost, but a significant investment in changing the interpersonal climate of your workplace. Others may challenge you to re-prioritize your current resources or find additional sources of funding. Still others may call for a community-wide plan to unite forces and take action.

Your center may have achieved many of the Model Work Standards, and others may seem within your grasp. But there are likely to be some which are unattainable within the current scope of your program. These standards, especially those that carry a high financial cost, are included not to frustrate you but to remind ourselves and others of our vision of a good child care job, our goals for change, and the need for

ACTIVITY

USING THE MODEL WORK STANDARDS

We recommend that as a group, the staff at your program work through the following process:

➧ **Assess your current working environment using the Model Work Standards.** You may choose to do this as a group—preferably the teaching staff and director together—or ask everyone to assess the program individually, and then come together to identify areas of consensus and disagreement. Looking at each standard, determine whether all staff agree that your program meets this particular goal. If not everyone agrees whether a certain standard has been met, it will be important to work toward understanding why the staff have varying perspectives on this subject.

➧ **Discuss higher and lower priorities for improvement.** For those standards which the program does not consistently meet, determine which are of higher and lower priority, using a process similar to that in step #1. While reaching consensus on level of priority is desirable, it is less important than agreeing whether a standard is consistently met.

➧ **Determine the cost for each of your top priorities.** It is important to place a dollar amount on the various goals you have set. Some programs decide how much money they can allocate or will raise to make changes (e.g., $5,000 for the coming year) and then select their top priority.

➧ **Make an action plan.** Ask each staff person to identify, among their high priorities, one to three standards which they want to work on achieving first. Then, rank the top one to three priorities that are agreed upon by all staff members. (Keep in mind that this is a time when significant class and cultural differences may emerge in terms of what various staff members need and want most.) You may want to start with an item that you believe will be fairly achievable but meaningful: for example, increasing the number of paid sick days. Your action plan should also include a time line, notes on what kinds of support and resources you will need to accomplish your goal, and information on who will take responsibility for certain tasks.

➧ **Document your progress.** This will help you evaluate, learn from and adapt strategies to sustain continued efforts.

➧ **Celebrate and broadcast your accomplishments.** Every victory, no matter how large or small, moves you closer to your goal of achieving good child care jobs.

greater investment in our nation's child care system. The standards can help us all to identify the gap between current child care work environments and those that are needed to truly create high-quality care for children.

As a working tool for setting goals to improve your current work environment, the Model Work Standards can engage both teaching staff and administration in developing an action plan for change. Programs in which teachers are represented by a union can also use them to assess the current collective bargaining agreement.

▮ ▮

This process—even if it's on a small scale, focused on solving a relatively simple problem in the work environment—is essentially the same process you will need to use in order to create a program-wide "action plan" for taking on turnover. After discussing the issues of recruitment and hiring, compensation, and substitutes in the following sections, we will return to the question of how to make a turnover action plan on page 138.

SECTION 2. RECRUITMENT AND HIRING: GETTING IT RIGHT FROM THE START

WANTED: Sensitive, caring, intelligent, energetic, well-organized, well-educated, friendly, cooperative person to plan and carry out an excellent program for young children. Train a new assistant teacher every six months; supervise substitutes and volunteers; work harmoniously with co-workers, administrators and parents. Long hours, no career ladder, minimal pay. Associate or Bachelor's degree preferred. Apply now!

If this job ad sounds familiar, you know that recruiting and hiring teaching staff for a child care program is one of the hardest jobs there is. But while there may be limits on what you can do at your own program level to come up with a perfect pool of job candidates, there are a variety of elements to your current process that could be helping or hindering your level of success.

Good hiring practices are a key part of preventing turnover, just as surely as poor hiring practices tend to fuel it. And in a participatory work environment, hiring is not the sole responsibility (or burden!) of administrators or boards of directors. Teaching staff should play a major role in recruitment and hiring, too: they not only have a personal stake in knowing who their co-workers will be, but first-hand knowledge, based on daily classroom practice, about what it takes to do the

> Teaching staff should play a major role in recruitment and hiring: they not only have a personal stake in the outcome, but first-hand knowledge of what it takes to do the job well.

job well. They also bear the brunt of bad hiring decisions, by facing the undue stress of orienting and working with staff who are inappropriate for the program—a level of stress that can easily make them want to leave the job themselves.

When your child care program takes the time to recruit and hire people who are skillful, knowledgeable and philosophically compatible, you are removing a major reason why people leave their jobs. But in our profession, wage levels often put a severe limit on the pool of available candidates. And we are often under such pressure to keep our programs staffed, and meet the proper adult-child ratios, that we keep hiring people we know are not likely to succeed and stay.

Hiring should never be an incidental or hasty process. It's often better—as many teachers themselves observed during our turnover trainings—to hire a

---

ACTIVITY

HIRING PROCESSES YOU'VE KNOWN

➠ Recall a hiring process that you have gone through yourself, or one that you have witnessed.

➠ List two or three things that were helpful or successful about the process.

➠ List two or three things that you would do differently.

➠ What implications does this experience have for your program's current recruitment and hiring practices? Which aspects of these practices would you like to change?

---

long-term substitute instead, and allow yourself enough time to make a better long-term staffing choice. A hiring strategy should not be dictated by desperation! Getting it right from the start can save your program time and money, and assure the quality and continuity of the services you provide. It shows that you take the job of child care teaching seriously, recognizing that not just anyone can do it. And it can help you save your energy to join with others in advocating for a better-funded, better-supported child care system, so that recruiting and retaining people in this field won't be so difficult in the future.

Often, you may feel that "there just aren't any good people out there," or that you can't recruit them because of your current pay scale. While these barriers are serious, there are a few nuts-and-bolts considerations that can help you make the best of the situation, and give your program an edge in recruitment and hiring. To have the best possible pool of applicants whenever job openings occur, your program should have an ongoing strategic recruitment and hiring plan, and a procedure for reviewing it from time to time. There are eight basic elements of such a plan:

- a statement of your program's philosophy

- an organizational chart

- job descriptions

- a competitive salary and benefits schedule

- a recruitment plan

- an interviewing and selection process

- an orientation procedure for new staff

- a probationary period.

WRITING A PROGRAM PHILOSOPHY STATEMENT

If you do not currently have a written statement of your child care program's philosophy, it may not be clear to a prospective staff person whether he or she would fit in with your program— and it may not be clear to you whether hiring this person would be a good fit. The statement should be simple and brief, and once it is drafted, it should be reviewed, approved and finalized with the full involvement of administrators, teaching staff and parents.

ACTIVITY

A PHILOSOPHY STATEMENT

One way to begin developing a philosophy statement is for all staff members to complete the following phrases, based on their own beliefs and values, and on their understanding of what the program stands for as a whole. These drafts should then be shared for comment and comparison.

Children learn best when...

The role of teachers/adults in children's learning is...

The ideal learning environment for children is...

The materials for children's learning should...

The role of culture in children's learning is...

The role of parents and family in children's learning is...

Next, drawing from each person's most valued beliefs about these issues, the staff as a whole, or a subgroup of volunteers, should draft a philosophy statement for the program, perhaps starting with the words, "We believe...." The statement should include something from each of the above areas, but it does not need to be limited to those words and concepts. Keep the statement as brief as possible; one page is definitely best.

Once your program has completed the statement, you will probably find that it also has other uses, such as recruiting new families, publicizing your program in the community, and writing to potential funders.

NOTE: As a separate activity, you can also ask job candidates during the interview process to complete these statements. Ask for concrete examples, so that you don't simply get canned early childhood education lingo such as, "Children learn through play." But remember not to give this exercise too much weight. Some candidates will be much more dynamic and creative in a classroom setting with children than they are at giving articulate answers to philosophical questions.

DEVELOPING AN ORGANIZATIONAL CHART

Child care programs need an organizational chart that identifies the roles necessary for running a quality program and the number of people needed in each role. It's helpful when an organizational chart also shows both "vertical" (supervisory) and "horizontal" (peer) role relationships. For a small center, an organizational chart can be very simple, but for a large program or a multi-site agency, it might be considerably more complex.

Particularly in a large program, a chart can help you see which roles are key to the program's continuity, and where staff might be shifted horizontally or vertically to support a vacancy while a hiring process is underway.

The chart should be distributed to all current and incoming staff, and discussed as a group, to assure that everyone understands the program's organizational structure. (See page 96.)

CREATING JOB DESCRIPTIONS

Clear and accurate job descriptions help everyone in a child care program understand their rights and responsibilities, and their place within the overall organizational structure. Even volunteers and substitutes should have a job description and/or a clear written agreement about what their tasks and roles will be.

Job descriptions are an essential part of matching openings with appro-priate applicants, and orienting newly-hired staff members to the work they will be doing. Remember that a job description should focus on the demands and requirements of the job itself, not on the personal style or skills of the staff member who is currently performing it. You can also take the opportunity of a job-turnover transition to review whether a particular job description is still accurate or should be changed. (See page 97.)

ESTABLISHING A COMPETITIVE SALARY AND BENEFITS SCHEDULE

Your program's compensation and benefits package can be your strongest recruitment tool, particularly if it gives you an edge over other programs in your area—or it could be your weakest, if you're paying the average "going rate" or less. A salary schedule is a way to formally set forth your system of compensation and reward. It classifies jobs according to their level of responsibility and complexity, and establishes a method to award salary increases consistently and fairly. Ideally, a salary schedule will express your program's priorities and values with regard to education, ongoing training, seniority, merit and other factors. It should be readily available to all staff.

If your program has a salary schedule, but it is out of synch with your priorities, you may be sending a confusing message which could stand in the way of attracting and retaining the staff

ACTIVITY

ORGANIZATIONAL CHART

To design an organizational chart, follow the steps described below. In the process, you might also want to indicate any aspects of the current structure that you would like to change. Administrative and teaching staff can all complete the questionnaire and compare their answers, looking for areas of agreement, disagreement and/or misunderstanding. (NOTE: Some software programs for managers and administrators also provide sample organizational charts.)

1. List every job category in your program and the number of positions there are in each category. For example: Teachers (6), Cook (1), Administrative Assistant (1), Director (1).

2. With this information, you can create various kinds of charts that will show the structure of the organization and specify the vertical and horizontal relationships between positions. You can use circles, rectangles or other shapes to show positions, and solid lines, broken lines or dots to show the relationships between them. Typically, solid lines are used to show direct relationships or lines of authority, and broken lines or dots indicate more indirect connections. Charts can have different levels of detail:

→ job categories and number of positions needed. A general organizational chart of this kind does not list the names of individual staff members in the program. Instead, it is intended to show the relationships between positions, not people.

→ all categories in the program, and the name of each staff member who holds a position in that category. Particularly in a large program, this more detailed chart can give a clearer idea of the staffing pattern of the organization and the relationships not only of positions but of staff members.

3. If you have a large program, studying the organizational chart can help you determine what are the key positions that must always be staffed for the sake of continuity, and which, if any, might be adequately combined with other positions temporarily while you seek to fill a vacancy. The entire staff should review the chart and give their input.

ACTIVITY

JOB DESCRIPTIONS

Use the outline below to develop a job description for each position in your program, or to revise existing job descriptions. These should be finalized only after consulting with the staff members who currently perform the particular jobs.

Position Title

Salary Range and Benefits

Qualifications

Responsibilities

Title of Immediate Supervisor

Work Schedule

you would like. Particularly if your program offers different salaries for the same job—or has a salary schedule which the administrators are secretive about—it could be sowing serious division and discontent. Or, if you don't have a salary schedule, prospective and current staff lack a blueprint about how to advance in the organization, which could undermine the sense of fairness and equity you need for fostering teamwork and high morale.

For a more detailed discussion of salary schedules and how to create them, see page 118.

OUTLINING A RECRUITMENT PROCESS

Imagine the kinds of people you would most like to work with at your child care program. Who are you looking for? What qualities should they possess? And how can you build a staff that reflects the cultural and linguistic diversity of your community?

At the same time, ask yourself why a job applicant should choose to work in your program. What makes your program unique or outstanding? What opportunities for professional advancement does it offer? What makes it a good place to work?

These basic questions will be easier to answer once you have agreed on your program's philosophy, and have a clear organizational chart and set of job descriptions. Your answers can then guide the kinds of recruitment activities you will conduct in order to find the people you want. (For more discussion of other topics related to recruitment challenges, see also "Improving Your Program's Substitute Policies," page 127, and "Beyond Individual Programs: Community Efforts to Take On Turnover," page 144.)

A recruitment plan has three basic components:

✓ an advertising and outreach plan, which should include specific plans for recruiting a culturally diverse staff,

✓ an application process, and

✓ a procedure for screening applicants.

Advertising and Outreach

There are a number of ways to advertise a job opening in child care, and different methods will work better in different communities. But most importantly, you have to feel confident and positive about the type of job and working conditions you are able to offer.

Resource and referral agencies can often help child care programs by posting job notices or referring potential applicants to programs that have openings. Many programs aim to build relationships with local community colleges, particularly with instructors of early childhood education classes. Many advertise in newspapers, on the radio or over the Internet, either periodically or on an ongoing basis; in some communities, a group of child care programs joins together to post a joint advertisement year-round. Some keep a running "recruitment list" or "staff waiting list" of people they have screened, and of substitutes, interns and volunteers who have worked at the program.

To recruit a diverse staff that reflects the families and community you serve, your program may also need to take "affirmative action"—examining your entry-level requirements, and allowing for more diverse pathways into child care employment. Educational requirements, in particular, often act as barriers for cultural communities that have long faced poverty, discrimination and poor schooling. To counteract these obstacles, your program could give consideration to specialized skill areas, such as bilingualism or work experience with communities of color—and make a commitment to strengthening the on-the-job training (including mentoring) your program provides. Some programs have also created new entry-

ACTIVITY

RECRUITMENT

Use the following questionnaire to develop your own recruitment process, or to evaluate and refine your existing process. Administrative and teaching staff can all complete the questionnaire and compare their answers, looking for areas of agreement, disagreement and/or misunderstanding.

➡ What are the qualities that a child care director/teacher/assistant teacher etc. should possess? (Examples: flexibility, humor, knowledge of child development, good listening skills.)

➡ What makes your program unique or outstanding? What professional opportunities does it offer? What makes it a good place to work?

➡ Develop an application form for your program. What will it include besides name, address and phone number? What kinds of background information will you ask for? (See page 102 for types of questions it is illegal to ask.)

➡ What other items will you require besides an application form? For example, a résumé, personal references, or transcripts or other records of education and training?

➡ Write a brief advertisement for a job opening at your program, including the basic information about responsibilities, work schedule, required education or experience, and where or how to apply. You may also wish to include salary and benefits information, and a closing date for applications.

➡ Where and how will you advertise this job opening? (Be sure that all staff members have input on places to target.)

➡ Describe your screening process. How will you narrow the number of applicants to those who will be selected for an interview? Who will be involved in the screening?

level job categories such as "floater teacher" or "relief care teacher" to help a more diverse pool of candidates enter the workforce.

Consider, too, your program's pro-

motion policies: namely, how well they provide options for current staff to move up the job ladder or advance their professional development in other ways. Are opportunities equal? Often, for example, a pattern can emerge in which women of color remain stuck at the assistant teacher or aide level, while European Americans, often with better access to higher education, continue to be hired from outside the program when teacher positions open up. Does the program make use of training resources in the community to help all interested staff move into new job roles when openings occur? Do you use substitute, student intern and volunteer positions effectively as springboards for moving into your program's regular workforce? And are teachers also rewarded for their extra efforts when they provide training and mentoring to assistant teachers and aides?

Applications

An application form elicits the basic information you need for determining whether a person should be considered for a job interview. Keep the form simple, limiting it to what you really need to know. Be aware, too, of the various kinds of questions it is illegal to ask on an application form or in an interview, and keep in mind that federal and state laws vary. (See page 102.)

Screening

Your screening process is a way of selecting which applicants should receive further consideration and be interviewed for a job. This can involve two parts: a set of criteria for evaluating application forms (e.g., Does the person have sufficient levels of preparation or experience for the job? Is his or her job experience in child care or a related field recent enough?); and a brief telephone or in-person interview of three to five questions that can be used to narrow down the number of people selected for a full interview. Decide also who will be involved in screening applicants: administrative staff, teaching staff, parents, and/or board members?

CONDUCTING INTERVIEWS AND MAKING HIRING DECISIONS

After you have narrowed the pool of available candidates, a classroom observation and an interview are the final ways of deciding which candidate will be most appropriate for the job, and has the qualities and skills you are looking for. Whenever possible, it should be program policy to include a staff member from the classroom concerned—usually the head teacher—in this observation and interviewing process.

Most programs ask all finalists to come for a classroom visit, during which time the candidate conducts an activity or works with the children for a certain period, and is observed by the director, teaching staff, and/or parents. Afterward, there should be time available for the candidate to meet with one or more of the observers (director, teacher, and/or parent) to discuss the visit and to answer any questions.

All finalists still under consideration are then given an interview. Your pro-

ACTIVITY

THE INTERVIEW AND HIRING PROCESS

Write a description of your interview and hiring process, including the following considerations. Administrative and teaching staff can all complete the questionnaire and compare their answers, looking for areas of agreement, disagreement and/or misunderstanding. People who have been hired recently may be able to give the best feedback on what has and hasn't worked well.

1. Who will be involved in observing candidates when they visit the classroom? Who will meet with them afterward to discuss the visit and answer any questions?

2. Who will be involved in interviewing candidates?

3. What general questions will you ask about the candidate's background, work habits and professional philosophy?

4. What situational questions will you ask, related to working with children, staff, parents and/or the community?

5. For each question, what are your benchmarks for an excellent, good, average or poor answer? (These should be established prior to the interviews, to assure that the hiring committee rates applicants objectively and fairly.)

6. Are you aware of the types of questions that you cannot legally ask in an interview? (See page 102.)

7. Which aspects of the job, if any, are negotiable between the program and the job applicant?

8. Who will make the final hiring decision? Who will be consulted?

9. How will candidates be notified of the hiring decision?

gram should have a standard list of general questions that it asks of all job candidates about their work styles, values, experience, qualifications and professional goals, as well as a few hypothetical questions about how they might respond to certain situations. These can then be adapted for particular situations. During the interview, you may also wish to review once more the job description for the position, the program's personnel policies and staff

WHAT QUESTIONS SHOULD NOT BE ASKED ON APPLICATION FORMS OR IN AN INTERVIEW?

If your program has fifteen or more employees, *federal employment discrimination laws* prohibit you from asking job applicants any questions that could be construed to show you are excluding individuals based on their race, sex, religion, national origin, color, age or disability. (For example: Job advertisements should avoid criteria such as "college student" or "recent college graduate," because they can be seen as excluding applicants on the basis of age.) Although it is sometimes difficult to discern what kinds of pre-offer inquiries are permissible, the following is some general guidance.

Job application forms may include questions about date of birth or sex, provided that these are for legitimate administrative reasons and not meant to exclude individuals based on their sex or age. Questions about race can be included if it is clear that a response is completely voluntary. Generally, job interview questions that are not directly related to an individual's ability to perform the job, but focus instead on his or her personal status, should be avoided.

You may not ask questions about an applicant's family responsibilities or plans to have children, or in the case of a female applicant, whether she is pregnant.

You may not, during the pre-offer stage, inquire about an applicant's health conditions or disability. You may, however, inquire whether an applicant can perform the essential functions of the job, and ask him or her to describe how they would perform those functions. After an offer is made, you may require all employees to take a test to determine whether they are physically or mentally able to perform the duties of a job, but the tests must be related to the actual job duties.

You may not ask an applicant about his or her religion. You should be careful about questions regarding an individual's availability to work on particular days, because such questions can be interpreted to show an attempt to exclude people of a particular religion. Employers have a duty to accommodate employees' religious beliefs, including time off for religious observances, unless this will cause undue hardship to the employer.

You may not refuse to hire someone for speaking English with an accent.

Please note, too, that in many states, *state employment discrimination laws* are more stringent than federal law. Check with the applicable agency in your state to be sure you know the provisions of these laws.

If you have a specific legal question, be sure to consult an attorney.or legal assistance organization. See also: *Rights in the Workplace: A Guide for Child Care Teachers* by the Center for the Child Care Workforce and the Worker Options Resource Center (CCW & WORC, 1997). ★

evaluation procedures, and especially your organizational and educational philosophy.

Finally, the program should have a clear policy about who makes final hiring decisions, who is consulted for input into hiring decisions, and how candidates are notified.

CONDUCTING AN ORIENTATION PROCEDURE FOR NEW STAFF

A well thought-out, written orientation procedure is critical for helping a staff member adjust to a new position, as well as helping the current staff, parents and children adjust to the new staff member. For example, is the person allowed a certain period to observe the operation of the program or classroom, and to get acquainted with the staff, parents and children, before she is expected to begin work? A workplace sends many signals about its culture and style by the way it receives a new person into a job—and this can have lasting effects on whether the match will be a successful one. A poor orientation procedure can undo all the work you've done on recruitment and hiring, but a positive one can make your program a place that a new staff member will want to stay in. (See activity below.)

ACTIVITY

ORIENTATION PROCEDURES

Answer the following questions to evaluate your current procedure for orienting new teaching staff members. In each case, ask whether your current process has been effective or needs improvement. Administrative and teaching staff can all complete the checklist and compare their answers, looking for areas of agreement, disagreement and/or misunderstanding. .

➡ How is a new staff person oriented to the job, and to the overall culture of the organization? How long does the formal orientation period last?

➡ How is the staff person introduced to the staff, parents and children?

➡ How is the staff person informed about the program's personnel policies and procedures?

➡ How is the staff person informed about the programs' probationary period and evaluation process?

ESTABLISHING A PROBATIONARY PERIOD

The probationary period is the amount of time that an employer gives a new staff person to demonstrate his or her ability to perform a job. While 90-day probationary periods are a typical practice, this is often not a long enough time to draw appropriate conclusions. Frequently, in child care, we feel so besieged by turnover that we feel lucky to retain new people at all, and as a result, we fail to take probation periods seriously. But some pro-

---

ACTIVITY

PROBATIONARY PERIODS

Use this questionnaire to evaluate and improve your program's use of probationary periods for new staff members. Administrative and teaching staff can all complete the questionnaire and compare their answers, looking for areas of agreement, disagreement and/or misunderstanding.

1. How long is your current probationary period?

___ 3 months   ___ 6 months   ___ 12 months   ___ other

If you feel that this is not giving you enough time to evaluate a new staff member effectively, choose a time period that will work better for you.

___ 3 months   ___ 6 months   ___ 12 months   ___ other

2. How does your program observe/monitor a probationary staff person's job performance?

Informal observation?   ___ yes   ___ no
___ daily   ___ weekly   ___ monthly
___ twice during the probationary period   ___ other

Formal written observation?   ___ yes   ___ no
___ once during the probationary period   ___ bimonthly
___ monthly   ___ other

If you feel that this is not giving you enough information to assess the staff person's performance and potential, choose a different option that will work better for you.

---

grams establish a six-month or one-year probationary period to allow themselves ample time to monitor, support and evaluate the performance of a new staff member.

An appropriate probationary support system consists of clear performance criteria; a tool for measuring levels of acceptable and unacceptable performance; ongoing observations of and feedback to the staff person; and, if appropriate, an individualized staff development plan that you expect the person to implement with the program's support. Such a system will also help you gather clear documentation in

3. For each staff position, who is responsible for supervising and monitoring that person's performance during the probationary period? Is this a satisfactory arrangement, or should any changes be made?

4. Does your evaluation process during the probationary period cover all the following areas?

___ compatibility with the program's philosophy

___ relationships with other staff

___ interactions with children

___ curriculum implementation skills

___ interactions with parents and the community

___ openness to continued professional development

5. Does your current probationary process create an atmosphere of open communication and partnership? Does it keep the new staff person informed of how her supervisor and others feel the probationary period is going, and allow her time and opportunities to work toward any needed improvements? If not, what changes would help?

the event that the new staff member's job performance is inadequate. You should thoroughly discuss the probationary period, the program's job performance expectations, and the criteria for measuring excellence with new employees during the final hiring stage and orientation process. (See activity, page 104.)

A performance-based assessment tool is often the best way to determine a staff member's ability to do a satisfactory job. There are a variety of such tools available to select from in our field, or your program can choose to design its own. Whichever assessment tool you use, it should be directly related to the staff member's job description, and should help you evaluate his/her:

➡ ability to work with children in developmentally appropriate and culturally sensitive ways;

➡ ability to implement the program's curriculum;

➡ compatibility with the philosophy of the organization;

➡ professionalism in interacting with staff, parents and the community; and

➡ willingness to continue learning and developing professionally.

■ ■ ■

In the following section, we discuss ways of improving compensation and developing more equitable salary schedules, to become better able to attract and retain skilled, qualified teachers for the child care field.

SECTION 3. IMPROVING COMPENSATION IN YOUR PROGRAM

Child care remains one of the lowest-paid jobs in our society, and low wages have been found to be the greatest single cause of turnover in our field. When most people hear just how low teacher wages are in a typical child care center, they immediately understand that there's a problem: How can you expect to hire someone on that? How can you expect them to stay? Helburn and her colleagues (1995), for example, compared the earnings of child care center teachers to those of other women in the labor force with similar levels of education, and estimated that the average teacher "foregoes" about $5,000 per year by working in child care. And if their comparison had also included male workers, this estimate of foregone wages would nearly double.

But it's one thing to recognize the problem of child care compensation, and quite another to solve it. Few programs, if any, have the resources to solve it on their own, because parent fees alone are very unlikely to cover the cost of running a high-quality program. And it remains a major obstacle that child care teachers and directors—the front-line practitioners who are actually running programs and caring for children on a daily basis—are rarely "at the table" when child care funding and policy decisions are being made (Whitebook, 1997).

But improving compensation in your program doesn't mean only raising employees' rate of pay, although that is very important in our field. It can also mean dealing with a variety of other policies and practices, such as:

✓ improving your benefits package to help you recruit and retain a more diverse workforce;

✓ examining which aspects of teachers' jobs are paid and unpaid;

✓ eliminating secrecy in the program about staff pay levels; and

✓ looking at what kind of formal salary schedule, if any, your program has developed.

Benefits can be an especially good place to begin. By shopping around, for example, the staff of one program in our Taking On Turnover training were able not only to secure better health coverage but save $2,400 a year—a fund which has now been redirected toward offering all staff an additional paid personal day per year.

Solving the dilemmas of low wages and high turnover will take unified action among many programs in many communities. And yet we cannot let the scope of the problem keep us from examining our own workplaces, and doing what we can to improve compensation and retain a dedicated, qualified staff. This chapter offers practical guidance on how to begin.

BARRIERS TO RAISING CHILD CARE WAGES

Before we can take action on better compensation, it can be useful to acknowledge the barriers we face—including the prevalent arguments in our society, whether they are spoken or not, against raising wages in child care. You have probably heard some version of the following before. You may have made some of these statements yourself.

➡ **The effect on parents.** "Raising wages will increase the fees and drive parents away." "It will increase the gap between more and less affluent parents." "Many parents will have to send their children to lower-quality care, or it will no longer be worth it for them to hold jobs."

➡ **No money.** "The economic facts are against us. We're competing against people who do this kind of work for free—children's parents and relatives." "It's a hopeless situation; it's always been this way." "Show me the money. Where is it?"

➡ **Competing priorities.** "Wage increases compete with putting more funds into staff training, the curriculum, the facility, and supplies and equipment." "Higher wages reduce profit."

➡ **The nature and value of the work.** "You have to do child care because you love it. You can't come in expecting to make good money."

"We'll have a situation where people are in it only for the money." "Child care isn't good for children anyway. They should be at home." "It's just a transitional job for young people passing through; they don't really need higher wages." "The current training and education requirements aren't high enough to justify high pay scales." "How do you measure success in this field? There's no clear end product. How do you prove that child care benefits children or society, so that the people providing care are worth more?" "Child care is not professional work."

> The average child care teacher "foregoes" $5,000 or more per year that she could earn in another field.

Now, recognizing these commonly-heard arguments, we may be in a better position to think more clearly about why child care staff should earn better compensation. (Many of the following rebuttals, in fact, were generated by participants in our Taking On Turnover training.)

➡ **Economic and social realities.** "The cost of living keeps going up, and child care wages should, too." "There's a difference between going into a field just for the money, and going into a deep hole for doing the work you love." "We have to be able to support our own families; many child care workers do have dependents to support." "Better wages would keep us from having to hold second jobs." "We're not living in the 1950s, and most women aren't staying at home, no matter how much some people might wish for that." "There is money available; it's a question of priorities. Our society makes decisions and choices every day about how our money is spent—like building more prisons instead of more schools."

➡ **Raising quality.** "At low wages, it's hard to attract the best and most skilled teachers." "High staff turnover means that children don't get the kind of care that helps them develop and learn. Children deserve to have adults who really know them and care about them." "Staff would be more conscientious and feel more professional if they earned what they deserve." "You can't teach self esteem to children if you don't have it yourself."

> **In a recent study of NAEYC-accredited centers, those who retained their highly-skilled teachers paid an average of $2.00 per hour more than other centers.**

"When we link training with better compensation, there's an incentive to keep learning." "A more stable workforce would be more organized and more visible—which would help ensure that caregiver issues such as wages were part of our nation's policy agenda."

➡ **Cost-effectiveness.** "We're spending too much money on recruiting, training and retraining new staff, and all the administrative costs associated with turnover, that we could be putting into better wages."

➡ **Research on child care quality.** "Research has shown that high-quality child care is a sound social investment." (Parents are able to enter and stay in the workforce; child care programs offer families partnership and support; children enter school better prepared for success in learning; good child care helps save money down the line on special education and remedial services.) "Wages are the crucial difference in child care quality." (In a recent study of NAEYC-accredited centers, those who retained their highly-skilled teachers paid an average of $2.00 per hour more than other centers. The study also found that, just as turnover tends to breed more turnover, an atmosphere of stability and staff retention leads to continued stability.) (Whitebook, Sakai & Howes, 1997.)

➡ **Parents as partners and advocates.** "Parents can be our allies in seeking more resources for our child care system." "While most parents can't pay more for child care, some could, through sliding fee scales or other systems." "There are other ways to raise child care funds besides raising parent fees." (In Military Child Care programs, system-wide resources are going into boosting wages and training opportunities, to cover the gap between parent fees and the true cost of quality. Some cities have local development ordinances that put money into child care. Employers can help, through models such as the Seattle Business-Child Care Partnership. A number of states are investing public funds in improving child care wages and training hand in hand, through such efforts as Child Care Wage$ in North Carolina, and the T.E.A.C.H. program in over five states.) (Bellm, Burton, Shukla & Whitebook, 1997.)

Chances are, you carry some version of both of these lists in your head: the status quo, and the vision of where you would like to go instead. And it is only when we recognize the barriers that our field has taken for granted for far too long, that we can begin taking action to move beyond them.

SETTING SHORT-TERM GOALS FOR YOUR PROGRAM

Despite the enormity of the child care compensation problem, there are a number of ways for centers to set and achieve short-term goals to boost staff salaries and benefits. Even small improvements that are within the grasp of many programs can raise morale and reduce turnover—especially when they go hand in hand with an organizational commitment to keep seeking further improvements over time.

One step is to make sure that your center has a salary schedule that sets *internal equity* within the program,

guaranteeing that people with the same qualifications receive the same pay. (See "Creating and Refining Salary Schedules" on page 118.) Others might be to institute a cost-of-living adjustment for staff if your center hasn't done so recently; to add another professional development or personal day per year; to begin paying staff for some regular but currently unpaid task; or to improve the center's policies of reimbursing staff for classroom supplies or transportation to training. Even if these seem small, any changes that encourage staff members to remain on the job for even one more year would make a huge difference for programs and children.

CREATING AN ANNUAL FUND

A significant barometer of a healthy or troubled workplace is how well it handles conversations about money. Are financial constraints and budgetary issues discussed openly? Do teaching staff members have input in setting budget priorities? One good model is for a center to make the commitment to:

➡ set aside a certain pool of money each year for improvements in compensation and/or staff development;

➡ take an annual survey of staff for suggestions on how to use the fund; and

➡ reach a decision as an entire staff on how the money should be spent.

For example: Should the center begin (or increase) a retirement/pension

66 Day to day, our biggest problem is a lack of paid preparation and meeting time for teachers. We need established times to evaluate the day, discuss the children's participation and/or individual needs, and formulate lesson plans. Often we find that the prep time we're given is dependent on other teachers watching the children. This means that children don't receive the attention their parents are paying for, and the teachers left in charge are resentful. They feel they are left to maintain 'crowd control' instead of teach, while their co-workers get to take care of their classrooms. And 'all bets are off' when someone is sick: no one gets prep time then.

Then there's the prep work: the cutting, pasting, cleaning, etc. The teachers who prep during class time are frowned upon: they're ignoring their primary responsibility, the children. The teachers who take the work home and do it on their own time are considered 'martyrs' who make the others look bad. Who's right? While I have long been in the 'martyr' category, I think that teachers are right not to work when they are not paid. Yet I take too much pride in what I do the let all the extras slide. 99

—TEACHER, BERKELEY, CALIF.

fund? Should there be more vacation time? An additional professional development day each year, or twice a year, for visiting other child care programs? A cost-of-living adjustment? A change in the center's health plan, or an increase in the percentage of the premiums that the center pays? If staff are not currently reimbursed for classroom supplies, or for transportation to required training events, can the center begin reimbursing them? Until you get specific ideas on the table, you can never move toward lasting change and meeting needs that the staff as a whole can agree on. Even in a financially strapped year when raises do not seem possible, there is surely some other concrete step that can be taken.

Since staff members may have very different priorities, all should be welcome to put proposals forward, and to do some research on what each idea would cost. Once everyone knows and understands the costs involved in each proposal, the staff can then discuss the top three to five priorities, and the level of participation throughout the process will help ensure that all can reach a decision or compromise they feel comfortable with. If your program is unionized, these discussions can be part of contract negotiations between the collective bargaining unit and center management.

PAID AND UNPAID WORK

The problem of regularly occurring unpaid work is a persistent one in many child care programs. At our training sessions, we have asked teachers and directors about tasks for which they currently are not paid but feel that they should be. Repeatedly, we have found that the two groups are in close agreement on these issues, and often, directors have wanted to offer more than teachers were asking for, even if they did not know how to pay for such improvements.

Use the checklist on this and the following pages to identify priority areas for change in your center.

ACTIVITY

CHECKLIST ON PAID AND UNPAID WORK

❑ **Classroom preparation and planning time**, as part of one's regular paid work schedule, is an essential part of good teaching. The Model Work Standards developed by the Center for the Child Care Workforce recommend at least two paid hours per week for preparation and planning time, before or after one's classroom shift, but ideally, one paid hour per day (CCW, 1998a). At present, teachers are too often expected to complete their classroom planning during breaks or nap time (forfeiting it when not all the children fall asleep), or in unpaid time at home. Too often, the result is insufficient planning and poorer-quality care. Whenever possible, centers should provide a separate staff room so that teaching staff can complete their preparation and planning with no children present.

Our current system:

What we would like to have:

❑ **Staff meetings** should be paid work time, and should occur frequently enough to ensure good communication and program planning. A commonly accepted standard is to hold weekly meetings for classroom teams (with briefer check-ins on a daily basis), and entire staff meetings at least once or twice per month.

Our current system:

What we would like to have:

❏ **Training and professional development activities** that staff are required to complete must (by law) be done on paid time.* Also, consider whether other kinds of "non-required" activities are paid or unpaid: for example, committee or Board work, or child care advocacy activities in the community?

Our current system:

What we would like to have:

❏ **Classroom and center clean-up**, whether on a daily basis or on a frequent or occasional weekend schedule, should come with additional pay if it is added on to teachers' regular hours. Alternatively, this task can be transferred to other paid or volunteer (e.g., parent) help. Anything beyond the kinds of moderate classroom clean-up that teachers can do with children's help should not be part of a staff member's regular teaching hours.

Our current system:

What we would like to have:

❏ **Social events**, such as pot-luck dinners with parents, should be paid time whenever staff members are expected or required to attend them.

Our current system:

What we would like to have:

❏ **Parent conferences** and **child assessments** should ideally be done during paid time that is explicitly set aside for these tasks—rather than the common practice of expecting teaching staff to complete them either during

* Recent rulings in several states by the Wage and Hour Division (W&HD) of the U.S. Department of Labor have advised child care programs that under the federal Fair Labor Standards Act, they must pay employees for all time spent in training that is mandated by the employer. In the case of state-mandated training, however, it remains hard to say whether the state or the employer is required to pay. Rulings in Florida, Minnesota and Texas have contradicted each other on this point, so it's best to contact the district or field office of W&HD in your area. Teachers who feel they may be owed pay for training should contact the W&HD, and could potentially receive back pay for up to three years. Wage and hours laws do not apply to administrators and supervisors.

lunch periods, breaks or nap time, or after hours, unpaid.

Our current system:

What we would like to have:

Late pick-up of children, which requires staff members to stay late, often involves a sizable fee paid to the center by the parent concerned; a five-minute grace period followed by a late fee of $1.00 per minute is a common practice. Many teachers, we have found, not only are not paid for this extra work time, but are expected to act as enforcers of the center policy with parents. Other centers, by contrast, award the late fee entirely to the person who stays late, rather than to the program, if she/he is an hourly wage-earning employee rather than an administrators or other salaried staff member.*

Our current system:

What we would like to have:

❏ **Mixed job roles**—for example, situations in which teaching staff also perform administrative tasks—should involve paid time at salary schedules appropriate for each.

Our current system:

What we would like to have:

❏ **Any other unpaid work items**.

Our current system:

What we would like to have:

* Note, however, that programs may not be able to charge such extra fees to parents who receive subsidized care. In that case, the program should be responsible for paying teaching staff for their additional time.

CALCULATING A SELF-SUFFICIENCY OR LIVING WAGE FOR YOUR COMMUNITY

The Model Work Standards recommend that the entry-level point on a child care program's salary scale, for teacher aide and teacher assistant jobs, should be a locally-determined 'self-sufficiency wage' or 'living wage.' At the upper end, over the long term if necessary, they also urge parity with elementary school teachers' salaries (Center for the Child Care Workforce, 1998a).

Information on teacher salaries in your area should be available from school district offices or teachers' unions. Determining local figures for an entry-level wage is also important since, due to wide variations in the cost of living among different parts of each state and the country as a whole, it is not possible or appropriate to recommend a single set of salary levels that would fit every community. But what do the terms 'self-sufficiency wage' and 'living wage' mean, and how can they be calculated?

There are several ways that communities have determined what is an adequate wage for someone to earn in their area, so as to get by without relying on any form of public or private assistance. This is then used as a rock-bottom, minimum figure in a variety of advocacy efforts. When it was first

developed, the federal minimum wage served this function of reflecting a decent subsistence level for a working American, but the minimum wage has long stopped keeping pace with inflation, and is now well below what is needed to stay economically afloat anywhere in the country.

Some communities have established Living Wage Campaigns which agree on a certain figure through a local consensus-building process, calculating the costs of various basic goods and services. The figure could be defined as a dollar amount or as a percentage of the federal poverty level. In one community, for example, the 'living wage' has been set by advocates at 110% of the poverty level for a family of four; in another, it has been set at $7.00 per hour if benefits are included, and $8.50 per hour if they are not. Welfare offices in your area may also have such information.

Wider Opportunities for Women (WOW), an anti-poverty project based in Washington, D.C., uses the term 'self-sufficiency wage,' and they have prepared county-by-county calculations in several states and the District of Columbia of a "Self-Sufficiency Standard": the hourly wage a worker (with a variety of different family configurations) needs to earn in order to be economically self-sufficient (Pearce, 1996). To reach these figures, WOW measured the average basic costs in

> **As much as half of the child care workforce earn an income at or below the poverty level, and as many as one-third earn the minimum wage.**

each county of housing, public transportation, food, licensed child care, one-third of health care expenses, and taxes. The figures assume that the worker is able to obtain all of these in the regular marketplace without outside assistance—i.e., without any use of public housing, welfare payments, child care subsidy, food banks, etc.

While it should not be difficult to argue that an entry-level worker in the child care field should earn such a self-sufficiency wage, the fact remains that many do not. It has been estimated that as much as half of the child care workforce earn an income at or below the poverty level, and as many as one-third earn the minimum wage. Calculating a more reasonable minimum level for your community is an important step to take—and it can become a very powerful tool for organizing, advocacy and education.

Family size is also an important variable. Setting a standard that is appropriate only for a single adult has serious pitfalls—it perpetuates the idea that only single (generally young) people can afford to work in child care, or that a child care teacher must have a partner or spouse who earns a better income and can take on a disproportionate share of a family's economic responsibilities. Instead, calculating a self-sufficiency wage for a family of three or four members would come closer to reflecting reality: namely, that a very high percentage of child care teachers and providers are working to support their families.

While it takes more work to engage in a community process of deciding on a 'living wage' or 'self-sufficiency wage' figure, rather than using a standard, one-size-fits-all number, it is really the only way to measure what a decent, minimum level of earnings should be where you live.

For more information on Living Wage Campaigns, contact the Public Policy Department, AFL-CIO, address, (202) 265-9573, or Jobs With Justice, 501 Third St. NW, Washington, DC 20001-2797; (202) 434-1106.

As of 1998, Wider Opportunities for Women has completed Self-Sufficiency Standards for California, District of Columbia, Illinois, Indiana, Iowa, Maryland (Montgomery and Prince George's Counties), Massachusetts, New York City, North Carolina, Pennsylvania, Texas and Virginia (City of Alexandria, and Arlington and Fairfax Counties). To learn more about the Standard or to develop one for your county or state, send a letter of inquiry to "Self-Sufficiency Standard" at: WOW, 815 15th Street, N.W., Suite 916, Washington, DC 20005; fax: (202) 638-4885; e-mail: info@w-o-w.org.

SAVING ON GOODS AND SERVICES THROUGH COOPERATIVE BUSINESS DEVELOPMENT

In some communities, either on their own or with the help of a resource and referral agency or other third party, child care centers are beginning to

COOPERATIVE BUSINESS DEVELOPMENT:
OPTIONS FOR CHILD CARE CENTERS*

FUNCTION	Our center currently shares this function with other centers	Our center would consider a joint effort/ purchase with other centers	Our center could provide this service for other centers
PERSONNEL-RELATED SERVICES			
Employee Benefit Administration	❑	❑	❑
Initial Screening	❑	❑	❑
Orientation	❑	❑	❑
Payroll	❑	❑	❑
Recruitment	❑	❑	❑
Training	❑	❑	❑
OTHER SHARED SERVICES AND STAFF			
Accounting	❑	❑	❑
Art, Music and Movement Teachers	❑	❑	❑
Audit	❑	❑	❑
Banking Charges	❑	❑	❑
Classroom Substitutes	❑	❑	❑
Clerical Assistance	❑	❑	❑
Financial Analysis	❑	❑	❑
Grant Writing and Development	❑	❑	❑
Janitorial Support	❑	❑	❑
Joint Purchases of Classroom Materials and Equipment	❑	❑	❑
Joint Purchases of Food	❑	❑	❑
Joint Purchases of Office Supplies	❑	❑	❑
Legal Advice	❑	❑	❑
Marketing	❑	❑	❑
Materials Development, e.g. Brochures	❑	❑	❑
Meal Preparation and Delivery Service	❑	❑	❑
Meeting Facilitation	❑	❑	❑
Parent Billing and Collections	❑	❑	❑
Professional Journals	❑	❑	❑
Psychological Counseling, Physical and Speech Therapy for Children	❑	❑	❑
Strategic Planning	❑	❑	❑
Translation Services	❑	❑	❑
INSURANCE PLANS			
Automobile/Vehicle	❑	❑	❑
Dental	❑	❑	❑
Disability	❑	❑	❑
Health	❑	❑	❑
Liability, Directors/Officers	❑	❑	❑
Liability, Professional	❑	❑	❑
Life	❑	❑	❑
Property	❑	❑	❑
Retirement	❑	❑	❑
Vision	❑	❑	❑
Workers Compensation	❑	❑	❑
OTHER			

* Adapted From Alameda Health Consortium, Cooperative Business Development Feasibility Study, 1996.

accrue savings—and directing them toward other priorities such as better staff compensation—by purchasing certain goods and services jointly with other centers. This practice is also known as "cooperative business development." The survey on page 117—which you could also distribute to other local centers—can help you identify possible advantages for your center in making such a development plan, and the areas in which you might join with other centers to cut costs.

➡ Which of the business functions listed on the chart might you consider moving out of your center to a centralized location, or purchasing from another organization, if you could save money and/or increase expertise? Also check any services which you could provide for other centers.

➡ Do you currently participate in any joint agreements with other centers or agencies to purchase services?

➡ Have you looked into negotiating discounts on any other goods and services?

➡ What advantages and/or disadvantages do you see in integrating certain services with other centers? What concerns, if any, do you have about sharing and/or centralizing functions with other centers?

> The goal of a fair and decent compensation policy in a child care program should be internal and external equity for all employees.

CREATING AND REFINING SALARY SCHEDULES

A salary schedule is a formal statement of the system of compensation and reward in a workplace. It classifies jobs according to their level of responsibility and complexity, and establishes a method to award salary increases consistently and fairly. Ideally, a salary schedule clearly expresses a program's priorities and values with regard to education, ongoing training, seniority, merit and other factors. It should be readily available to all center staff.

If your center has a salary schedule, but it is out of synch with your program priorities, you may be sending a confusing message to employees which could stand in the way of attracting and retaining the staff you would like. If you don't have one, staff lack a blueprint about how to advance in the organization, which could undermine the sense of fairness and equity that is essential for fostering teamwork and high staff morale.

Creating a Salary Schedule

1. CONDUCT A TASK ANALYSIS FOR EACH JOB IN THE CENTER.

Staff input is critical here. All employees should provide a detailed list of the tasks which comprise their jobs, and the frequency with which they perform each of them. Include any decision-making responsibilities. These lists should be reviewed and analyzed with each staff person to determine whether any duties should be changed.

2. DEVELOP JOB DESCRIPTIONS FOR EACH POSITION.

A job description defines a task within the center that needs to be done, not the individual who holds the job. See page 95 for guidance in developing job descriptions.

3. ESTABLISH A JOB CLASSIFICATION SYSTEM.

Next, compare jobs in relation to each other and group them according to difficulty, regardless of dissimilar functions. These categories should then be ranked in order of their complexity, level of responsibility, and amount of training and education required. Five to seven categories usually allow for enough diversity without being too cumbersome. It is more manageable to set salary ranges for entire categories than for individual positions within a center. Under such a system, each job in a given category would have the same dollar value as every other in that category.

The size of the gaps between starting salaries should accurately represent how positions fit into the agency structure. An unreasonable gap (e.g., directors earning twice as much as head teachers) will be reinforced over time if raises are based on a percentage. For example: an annual three-percent raise would amount to $1,200 for someone earning $40,000 per year, but only

$600 for someone earning $20,000. People on the lower end may resent the substantially lower dollar amounts of their raises.

On the other hand, if increases are given as fixed amounts (such as an annual $300 raise), the ratios between categories will change and the gap will be narrowed, but those who have reached the higher end of the scale may be dissatisfied with raises that reflect a lower percentage of their salary than those for staff with less experience, seniority and responsibility. When choosing the type of increase to be offered, aim for salary differentials that are fair reflections of the nature of the work.

Because both types of raises have certain drawbacks, you might wish to alternate which type you use, and review your policies periodically to make sure that they feel equitable to all.

4. ASSESS HOW CENTER WAGES COMPARE TO THE COST OF LIVING IN THE COMMUNITY.

Typically, most industries look at the "going rate" for labor in their communities in order to establish competitive wage scales. You can conduct your own informal wage survey by checking the newspapers, telephoning other centers, and looking at job announcements at local agencies. There may also have been a salary survey completed in your community in recent years; check with the Center for the Child Care Workforce, or your local child care resource and referral agency or early childhood association. In child care, however, the status quo is usually not an adequate wage. Comparability to other child care programs will do you little good if other centers are also having difficulty attracting and keeping qualified staff.

Ultimately, the goal of a fair and decent compensation policy in a child care center should be to establish both *internal* and *external* equity for all employees—that is, to set wage scales that are fair to everyone within the center, and that are in line with what others in the community earn with comparable levels of education and responsibility. If you or others have calculated a self-sufficiency or living wage for your area, this can be the standard for entry-level jobs. And as suggested above, child care teacher salaries should ideally reach parity with the earnings of elementary school teachers.* While many elementary school teachers are not paid what they deserve, either, the "comparable worth" goal of bringing child care salaries in line with those of other teachers is a valuable standard to set for our field—and for many, unfortunately, a still-distant one.

5. ESTABLISH A STEP SYSTEM FOR EACH JOB CLASSIFICATION.

A step system establishes variations in pay, and an upper limit, for each job category on the salary schedule. The base or beginning salary for a position

---

* Based on these principles, CCW has developed statewide child care compensation guidelines for the California Department of Education (Burton & Whitebook, 1998).

can be offered to an applicant who meets the minimum level of education and experience for the job, while a more qualified applicant might be offered the position at a higher salary.

To ensure fairness, limit the maximum number of steps above the base salary which will be offered to new job candidates, no matter how qualified they are. (The maximum might be two or three steps.) In addition, re-examine your program's policy on promoting from within. Perhaps the commitment to offering job advancement to existing staff can be strengthened, giving employees the opportunity to learn new skills and assume greater responsibility without leaving the agency.

Base salaries and raises should be reviewed annually, and adjusted to reflect the changing marketplace, even if the classification system remains the same.

Salary Increases: When and Why

Most salary increases occur annually, although every six months is also possible. What matters most is that all staff members know when to expect a review and/or an increase, and that the procedure should take place on time.

Most organizations opt for one of four systems for awarding salary increases—rewards for length of service, cost-of-living adjustments, rewards for professional development, or merit raises—or a combination of these. Each has its pros and cons.

A system based on *length of service* offers automatic increases—usually one

ACTIVITY

WHAT SHOULD BE THE BASIS FOR STAFF COMPENSATION AND REWARD?

A. WHAT YOU BELIEVE

STAFF QUALITIES	Rank (1 = most important 10 = least important)	Weight your top four (100 points total)
Seniority: years in your center	☐	☐
Experience in early childhood settings	☐	☐
Experience in a child care program similar to yours	☐	☐
College units in early childhood education or child development	☐	☐
Permits or credentials (e.g., Child Development Associate)	☐	☐
College degrees in early childhood education or child development	☐	☐
Informal training in child care-related topics	☐	☐
Units or degrees in other non-related fields	☐	☐
Job performance ("merit")	☐	☐
Bilingualism	☐	☐
Other?	☐	☐

STEPS:

1) Rank these items from one to ten, according to the qualities you consider most important for staff in your program.

2) Next, look at the top four qualities you have selected. Weight your top four in order of importance, using a 100-point system. For example, if experience in early childhood programs similar to yours heavily outweighs all others, it might receive 50-75 points, while a lesser priority might receive 10-25 points, etc. Total points should equal 100.

ACTIVITY

WHAT SHOULD BE THE BASIS FOR STAFF COMPENSATION AND REWARD?

B. WHAT YOU THINK YOUR CO-WORKERS BELIEVE

STAFF QUALITIES	Rank (1 = most important 10 = least important)	Weight your top four (100 points total)
Seniority: years in your center	☐	☐
Experience in early childhood settings	☐	☐
Experience in a child care program similar to yours	☐	☐
College units in early childhood education or child development	☐	☐
Permits or credentials (e.g., Child Development Associate)	☐	☐
College degrees in early childhood education or child development	☐	☐
Informal training in child care-related topics	☐	☐
Units or degrees in other non-related fields	☐	☐
Job performance ("merit")	☐	☐
Bilingualism	☐	☐
Other?	☐	☐

STEPS:

1) Rank these items on a scale of 1 to 10, as before, but according to how you think your co-workers would rank them. If you feel that they disagree among themselves about what should be rewarded, indicate these differences in the second column.

2) Compare answers with your co-workers, to see how accurately you have assessed each other's beliefs and value systems about compensation and reward.

step in a salary range—every six to twelve months, based on the premise that the worth of employees increases as they gain skills, knowledge and experience over time. Some programs may find that it is more difficult to weed out unsatisfactory employees with this type of system. A comprehensive evaluation system, kept separate from raises, could be a more effective way to monitor and improve professional growth. Automatic increases, however, do assure staff that their value is noted and will be acknowledged in predictable increments at predictable times. In an historically underpaid field such as child care, automatic increases acknowledge the importance of upgrading salaries for all who work in the field.

Cost-of-living raises might best be used to supplement an existing system of salary increases, rather than as an exclusive means. While such raises are desirable, staff members who rely on them may find that their amount is often unpredictable. Nor is this a very equitable pay increase system, as not everyone is equally affected by changes in the cost of living. Programs that wish to respond to the changing economy might either give lump sum awards to staff, exclusive of their annual salary increases, or adjust base salaries and corresponding steps to reflect changes in the cost of living.

Rewards for *professional development* can also be used as a supplementary system. Not every staff member has equal opportunities to obtain additional education, regardless of their

desire to do so. If additional training is a priority for the position, the center can encourage participation by offering in-service training, release time to attend classes, or tuition stipends for staff.

Merit raises are often used in the private sector, but can be applied to other settings. Merit systems use financial reward as an incentive to continue good performance and to encourage others to work toward their maximum potential. Theoretically, employees who are performing below par would be denied increases until they improve, and raises would be given periodically only to the deserving.

A merit system demands a lot of attention to effective supervision and feedback. Supervisors need to be well-trained in evaluation, observation and communication. Staff members who fail to receive merit raises will justifiably want clear guidance on how to secure a raise in the future. An employee must be given very specific instructions which will allow his or her improvement to be measurable. Some agencies develop objective criteria as the basis for merit increases in order to eliminate potential bad feelings about evaluation.

As with most systems which rely on human judgment, merit raises are always open to question, and can lead to resentment and divisiveness that are highly unproductive. If you decide to use such a system, all staff should be part of setting the performance standards serving as a basis for raises, and the standards should be understood and accepted by all.

BUILDING SALARY SCHEDULES: TWO CASE EXAMPLES

Example 1. The Cottonwood School

The Cottonwood School offers preschool, kindergarten and school-age programs. Preschool teachers have responsibilities for meeting with parents, documenting the development of the children in their classrooms, and supervising an assistant teacher and an aide. The school-age program teachers have similar responsibilities, in addition to helping children with homework. The kindergarten classroom has a team-teaching system in which teachers do not supervise other staff, but are responsible for coordinating their activities with other team members; they also have more extensive responsibilities for reporting to parents on children's progress in completing the kindergarten curriculum.

Although the school has set certain requirements for all staff positions, there is no formal salary schedule in place. Head teachers must have an A.A. degree in early childhood education, child development or a related field; assistant teachers must have completed 12 units; and aides must be enrolled in a unit-bearing program. Inservice training is offered on a voluntary basis. All employees who work 20 hours or more per week receive full benefits.

Julie, a part-time teacher in the school-age program, who has been at the school for seven years, started out as an aide with no course units in early childhood education, gradually completed an A.A. degree, and now qualifies as a head teacher. She has recently taken on the additional project of coordinating and improving the school's library of materials for children and teachers. Jan, a full-day preschool teacher who has a B.A. in child development, has been with the school for two years and is frustrated by her pay level. Marsha, a full-day, certified kindergarten teacher, is well aware that she earns much less at the Cottonwood School than she would in the public schools. Assistants and aides at the school have not expressed frustration and appear more satisfied with their salaries and benefits.

The director has attempted to keep staff morale high by offering a relatively generous benefits package, but now realizes that the school should develop a salary schedule. How should the salary schedule be structured? How should the teaching staff's varying levels of education, tenure and experience be rewarded?

Example 2. Nelson County School District Child Development Centers

The program director of the Nelson County School District Child Development Centers developed a salary schedule five years ago for all child care teaching staff and other employees in 50 sites around the county. The salary schedule includes job descriptions for all nine positions and a five-tiered classification system, as follows:

➡ CLASS I: $5.50 - $7.50 per hour

aide: assists classroom staff in caring for children.

driver: transports children and staff as required.

requirements: high school degree or equivalency

➡ CLASS II: $7.00- $9.00 per hour

health aide: presents information on health practices for staff and children.

assistant teacher: assists classroom staff in caring for children; plans activities for children under the supervision of teachers.

cook: prepares meals for children and staff; purchases food for program.

requirements: 6 units, or current enrollment, in a credit-bearing early childhood education/ Child Development unit-bearing program

➡ CLASS III: $10.00 - $14.00 per hour or $18,200 - $25,480 per year

teacher: responsible for group of children; supervises assistants and aides.

social worker: works individually and in small groups with children.

requirements: teacher required to have state early childhood education credential; social worker must have a B.A. degree in social work or related field.

➡ CLASS IV: $15.00 - $18.00 per hour or $27,300- $32,760 per year

site supervisor: responsible for the administration of site; supervises, hires/fires, and conducts evaluations of teachers and other employees at site.

requirements: state credential for child care administrator; B.A. in early childhood education, child development or related field; and two years' child care teaching experience.

➡ CLASS V: $20.00 - $30.00 per hour or $41,600 - $62,400 per year

program director: responsible for the administration and oversight of all sites; supervises, hires/fires and conducts evaluations of site supervisors.

requirements: state credential for child care administrator; B.A. in early childhood education or child development; five years' administrative experience; two years' child care teaching experience.

Salaries and benefits in School District programs are higher than in average child care programs in the community, and the agency has had relatively little difficulty in attracting and retaining staff, with an annual turnover rate of less than 10 percent. Staff have generally been happy with the salary schedule, believing that it fairly rewards staff for different levels of responsibility and education.

Several issues, however, have surfaced during the past year, suggesting to the program director and many of the staff that the salary schedule should be revised.

First, compliance with the state's new child care professional development system is now mandatory for all state-funded programs. The system includes several new requirements: all staff at the assistant level and above, for example, are required to complete professional development units. It has also has introduced several new job classifications, such as "master teachers." Aides are not included in the new system, and assistant teachers can only remain assistants for a limited time before they must meet the requirements of teachers. As a result, the school district's job descriptions and salary schedule are not fully in line with the new requirements.

Another issue concerns the annual cost-of-living adjustments (COLAs) which the district implemented four years ago. The COLAs are calculated as a percentage of employees' income, with the result that higher-wage

---

A ACTIVITY

BUILDING A SALARY SCHEDULE

We have provided the above case examples to stimulate your thinking about some of the issues involved in salary schedules. Now, following the steps we described in more detail beginning on page 118, create a salary schedule for your own program.

➡ Conduct a task analysis for each job in the center.

➡ Develop job descriptions for each position. (You may have already done so in working with the previous chapter on Recruitment and Hiring.)

➡ Establish a job classification system.

➡ Assess how center wages compare to the cost of living in the community.

➡ Establish a step system for each job classification.

➡ Determine when and why salary increases are offered.

---

employees have gained a much larger increase over time than lower-wage employees, and the gap in salaries between the two groups has increased dramatically. The union representing the aides, drivers, assistants and health aides is especially concerned about the discrepancy.

Finally, mandatory class size reduction in elementary school classrooms has created an opportunity and an incentive for B.A.-level preschool teachers to leave the child development centers and move into the public elementary schools, where they can earn from $28,000 to $50,000 per year.

The program director has gathered a committee of employees representing each job position in the child development sites to begin the process of revising the salary schedule. Her budget for salaries and benefits has not increased

this year, except for the money earmarked for cost-of-living increases. What steps should she and the employee representatives take to revise the salary schedule?

■ ■ ■

As administrative and teaching staff in your program take action together to improve compensation, we hope you will find that you can make more progress than you previously thought was possible. We also expect that you will come up against the limits of what you can do alone—but hope that you will now feel more energized to join with others to take longer-term action for worthy wages in child care. See Part 4, "Beyond Individual Programs: Community Efforts to Take on Turnover," for more ideas.

SECTION 4. IMPROVING YOUR PROGRAM'S SUBSTITUTE POLICIES

Child care is not the kind of service that can simply carry on with fewer staff when one or more teachers are away, or during the transition between a staff member's departure and the hiring of a replacement. But child care is perhaps the only service industry that lacks a reliable, community-wide infrastructure for recruiting and obtaining substitutes as needed—such as nurses' registries in the medical profession, or school substitute programs in public school districts.

As the demand for child care services grows, and as skilled and unskilled teachers alike continue to leave their jobs, the problems of finding and retaining qualified substitutes are becoming more acute in many communities. As one of the most difficult "stress points" in our field, in fact, the substitute dilemma is as good a barometer as any of the instability of our child care system.

In our Taking On Turnover training sessions, we have heard many indications of the desperation and lack of control about substitute issues that child care programs are experiencing: reports of feeling forced to pay substitutes a higher wage than permanent staff members, for example, or paying high finders' fees and hourly rates to profit-making substitute placement agencies—even when these subs are not well-screened or well-qualified—

> **The substitute dilemma is as good a barometer as any of the instability of our child care system.**

because there seems to be nowhere else to look. The scarcity of substitutes often puts programs in direct competition with each other, too, so that it becomes hard to work together on solving these issues. (More than one director at our trainings admitted not sharing the names of her best substitutes with colleagues!)

Yet a workable substitute system, and a stable pool of substitutes, are critical for reducing stress among staff and promoting consistent care for children. Reliable substitutes help create smoother transitions whenever turnover happens, and they are essential for allowing staff to have adequate vacation and sick leave.

Our approach to substitute issues, like our approach to turnover in general, involves two levels of work: improvements that can be made within individual programs, and broader community solutions that involve organizing and advocacy beyond one's workplace. While solving the substitute problem may mean linking with other child care programs and agencies, or even creating some kind of community-wide substitute system (see Part 4, page 154), there are several steps you can take to improve your program's procedures and make the best use of available substitutes. Clarifying your procedures, and making sure they are workable and fair for both staff and substitutes, are useful places to begin.

ASSESSING YOUR CURRENT SUBSTITUTE SYSTEM

"Substitute system?" you may ask. "We don't have a substitute system!" But in that case, the lack of one is also a "system." It's important to start by looking at how your program handles both anticipated and unexpected staff absences, and what it does to find substitutes when they're needed.

Evaluating your system may help you see that substitute problems affect various staff members differently, and that your current procedures are workable for some people but not others—the teacher who is sick, for example, or the director whose regular job goes undone whenever she has to fill in for teachers in the classroom.

To assess your current substitute system, fill out the worksheet on page 129:

➡ on your own;

➡ as a group in a staff meeting; and/or

➡ with people from other child care programs, as a way of comparing systems and experiences.

DEFINING RESPONSIBILITIES

Whose job is it in your program to arrange for substitutes when a staff member is sick? Make sure that all permanent staff members agree on the

answer! In our turnover trainings, we repeatedly found that this was one of the hottest issues among center-based teaching staff. We strongly recommend that it not be the sick person; she or he should be resting instead of taking on more work duties, especially a duty that can be so stressful. A common result of asking teachers to arrange for their own substitutes is that they go to work sick rather than face such an ordeal. Perhaps the responsibility for arranging substitutes can be rotated periodically rather than falling on one person. But we also strongly recommend that serving as "dispatcher" be a paid activity—not one more extra, after-hours, thankless job.

Frequently, the substitute shortage discourages both teachers and directors from taking their well-earned and much-needed leave time. But centers should develop an adequate substitute budget that allows for decent wages for subs, and clear policies and procedures, in order to encourage staff to take the sick and vacation time they deserve, and to allow them to participate in professional development activities outside the center. The alternatives may be staff burnout or a serious illness which should have been cared for sooner. A smoothly operating substitute system will also make it easier for people to re-enter when they have been absent. If the thankless job of scheduling substitutes remains a "hot potato," the person who has been away can often be the target for much of the tension that has accumulated in her absence.

ACTIVITY

YOUR SUBSTITUTE SYSTEM

1. Describe how your program currently recruits, orients, arranges and evaluates substitutes:

a) during unexpected absences

b) during anticipated absences, such as vacations and other annual leave

2. Identify the strengths and weaknesses of your current substitute system from the perspectives of the director, the sick or absent teaching staff, the teaching staff in attendance, the substitutes themselves, and the parents and children. If you are not sure how people in different roles would evaluate your current arrangement, ask for their opinions.

Role	Strengths of current system	Weaknesses of current system
Director		
Sick or absent teaching staff		
Teaching staff in attendance		
Substitutes		
Parents		
Children		

3. If you could change three things about your current substitute system, what would they be, in order of priority?

Larger child care programs are often able to employ part-time or full-time substitutes to rotate among classrooms. Other programs find it helpful to share a rotating substitute with one or more other local centers, allowing each center some guaranteed coverage and providing dependable employment for the sub. If no one is absent on your scheduled day, the substitute could allow time for the regular staff to attend to planning or parent conferences, or to take long-overdue compensatory time.

ESTIMATING SUBSTITUTE COSTS AND NEEDS FOR YOUR PROGRAM

It is a particularly serious problem that child care programs are often quite under-budgeted when it comes to substitute teachers. Funds for paying substitutes should be specifically included in a program's operating budget, and should only be spent for other purposes if there is a surplus at the end of the year. In our turnover trainings, once directors and teachers calculated their substitute costs and needs over several months or a year, many came to feel that their programs were chronically understaffed. They recognized that there will always be a need for occasional substitutes to cover unexpected illnesses, but what they really could use is an additional person or more on staff.

> Once directors and teachers calculate their substitute costs and needs, many come to feel that their programs are chronically understaffed.

Better-quality centers—and centers that experience less staff stress during times of turnover—often hire "floaters" or "permanent subs" to cover scheduled leave time such as vacations, training and orientation periods, and professional development days. While this may sound like a luxury, many centers have found that this is a full-time need for keeping their programs not only fully staffed and running smoothly, but also operating at full capacity. A vicious cycle can develop: centers with insufficient funding remain understaffed, which contributes to under-enrollment, which in turn undermines funding and places the center in jeopardy of closing.

Use the worksheet on pages 131-133 to estimate your own substitute costs and needs. The information you draw from it may be valuable for identifying staffing changes you should make, or for promoting such changes with your management or board of directors.

HIRING SUBSTITUTES

People often say that "a good sub is hard to find." Unfortunately, finding a good job as a substitute can be just as difficult. The lack of value placed on child care jobs in general is magnified for the job of substituting. It is often seen as the most unskilled position in a center, and staffed accordingly, rather

ACTIVITY

ESTIMATING SUBSTITUTE COSTS AND NEEDS

INSTRUCTIONS: This worksheet is designed to help you assess whether your current substitute budget adequately reflects your program's need for coverage. You will probably need to estimate average pay rates for some positions, since the same job may be held by people at different pay scales, based on their qualifications and tenure. When the time comes to prepare your next annual program budget, you will probably want to calculate these costs more precisely.

Once you have completed the worksheets, compare your grand total to the amount allocated in your annual budget for substitutes. Are you under- or over-budgeted for this item?

Also, compare the grand total with the cost of hiring one or more permanent, full- or part-time substitutes or "floaters" for your center. Floaters will not eliminate the need for an occasional sub, such as when several staff are ill at the same time, but can address many of the coverage needs for planned absences. Floaters can also be particularly helpful when working with infants and toddlers, because babies' comfort and well-being relies so heavily on familiarity with their caregivers. Would such an arrangement be less costly or less stressful?

Indirect Substitute Costs

Estimate your annual expenditures related to substitutes in the following areas:

A) Advertising _____
B) Screening and interviewing _____
C) Orientation _____
D) Other _____

Add these four figures to calculate:
Total annual indirect costs for substitutes _____

Direct Substitute Costs

SECTION 1

A) Number of teachers in the center receiving
   paid sick leave* _____

B) Number of paid sick days per year allotted
   per teacher _____

C) Number of teachers in the center receiving
   paid annual leave _____

D) Number of paid annual leave days allotted per
   teacher during times when the center is open** _____

- Multiply A x B _____
- Multiply C x D _____
- Add the totals to calculate:

Total days of substitute coverage needed per
year for teachers' paid annual and sick leave _____

SECTION 2

D) Number of assistant teachers or aides
   receiving paid sick leave* _____

E) Number of paid sick days per year allotted
   per assistant teacher or aide _____

F) Number of assistant teachers or aides
   receiving paid annual leave _____

G) Number of paid annual leave days allotted
   per assistant teacher or aide when
   the center is open** _____

- Multiply D x E _____
- Multiply F x G _____
- Add the totals to calculate:

Total days of substitute coverage needed per
year for assistant teachers' and aides'
paid annual and leave _____

* Some centers combine sick and annual leave, often calling it personal leave. The point here is to capture the number of days for which substitutes are likely to be needed during the year, and your calculations should reflect your program's situation. If your center's policies permit staff to carry over sick or annual leave to the next year, be sure that you have adequately budgeted for the possibility that someone may spend down their accrued leave. You might add that need for coverage in Section 3 below if you anticipate a long absence by one or more staff members, due to pregnancy, scheduled surgery, etc.

** If your center closes for any period of time—e.g., during the Winter holidays—and teaching staff are paid for vacation during this time, you would not have to cover their absence with a substitute. Similarly, paid holidays are not included here because most programs are closed. If your staff receive floating holidays (i.e., they can choose to take a holiday on a day when the center is open), include the number of days in Section 3 below.

SECTION 3

H) Number of additional paid days for training,
other professional development activities,
meetings, conferences with parents, floating
holidays, etc. allotted per teacher   _____

I) Number of such days allotted per assistant
teacher or aide   _____

J) Estimated number of additional days of
coverage for unplanned absences
(e.g., staff member who exceeds allocated
sick leave, etc.)   _____

• Add H, I and J to calculate:
Total days of additional substitute
coverage needed per year   _____

• Add the three totals (from Section 1, 2 and 3)
above to determine:
**Total days of substitute coverage needed
per year at your center**   _____

• Multiply this sum by the daily rate* your center
pays for substitutes, including payroll taxes:
total days _____ x daily sub rate _____
to calculate:
Total annual direct costs for substitutes   _____

Add this total to the "total annual indirect
costs" above to calculate:
TOTAL ANNUAL COSTS FOR SUBSTITUTES   _____

* Substitute pay rates: If you use an hourly rate for substitutes, you will have to determine a daily rate
or calculate the number of hours vs. days) you will need a substitute. If your center pays different
rates for substitutes depending on how long they have worked in your program, or their
qualifications, estimate an average sub rate or calculate the costs separately for number of days at
different rates. If you use part-time staff as subs, remember to budget them at their rate of pay, rather
than at the sub rate which is likely to be different.

ACTIVITY
ESTIMATING COVERAGE NEEDED FOR STAFF BREAKS

When coverage is tight, staff often sacrifice their breaks—a practice that is both illegal and unhealthy for everyone involved. In thinking about your additional staffing needs, you might also calculate the amount of coverage your center requires to ensure breaks for all staff. Although an extra person cannot relieve each staff member during the day, the calculations may be useful in your discussions with other staff and your Board or administration to educate them about staffing needs and to assist in planning.

A) Number of teaching staff on site per day working
shifts that qualify for breaks   _____
B) Average number of breaks per staff member per day   _____
C) Average length of break (in minutes)   _____

• Multiply A x B x C to calculate total daily
break times in minutes   _____

• Divide the total by 60 to calculate total hours
of daily coverage needed for staff breaks   _____

• Multiply this figure by the number of days
per year the center is open   _____

• Divide that figure by the number of hours
per day the center is open, to calculate:
**Total days of staff time needed per year for
break time coverage**   _____

than being given the consideration it deserves. If anything, substituting should perhaps be reserved for more-skilled, rather than less-skilled, child care workers. At the very least, child care programs must clarify what level of skill is needed by a replacement staff person, recognizing that most substitutes with higher than entry-level qualifications will not work for entry-level pay. (In some states, it is necessary to hire substitutes with different qualifica-

tions, depending on the absent staff member being replaced. Someone qualified to be an aide, for example, could not substitute for a teacher, if a teacher-qualified person is required for meeting licensing requirements.)

When hiring a substitute for the first time, be sure to have some interview questions ready, especially if your sub list comes from a referral program that does not screen or train the substitutes. Arrange a brief meeting and/or a classroom visit before the substitute works in the center; ideally, the person should be paid for the visit at the regular rate.

If a visit is impossible, conduct a brief interview over the phone. Ask about the person's education and exprience; which age groups they have worked with and which they prefer; and what kinds of activities they like to do with children. Keep the questions simple and few; this is not an interview for a permanent staff position! But do make the interview more than perfunctory: substituting in a child care center is hard work, and the best substitutes generally have some group child care experience that they can tell you about. It's not easy to enter a strange classroom and be immediately helpful to the children and the other staff, especially when working with infants and toddlers, and these skills should not be taken for granted.

Be sure, too, to give the substitute thorough information: the name and location of the program, the hours or days of work, the pay procedure, the age group he or she will work with, and the person to report to upon arrival. A substitute should arrive a bit early to allow for some preliminary communication—with a co-teacher or other designated person—which can improve the course of the entire day or shift. The designated person should be somebody who can take the substitute on a tour, introduce her to other staff, and provide a general orientation.

ORIENTATION AND SUPERVISION: TIPS FOR WORKING WITH SUBSTITUTES

Retaining good substitutes is an important investment, so once your child care center has found good substitutes, how do you keep them? A group of substitutes in Berkeley, California got together and talked about what they have liked and disliked about their subbing experiences. Their comments point out many ways that centers could improve their substitute policies.

Several substitutes said they liked the flexibility of the job, the variety, and the perspective that comes from working in a number of different programs. Some considered it an ideal kind of child care training. There was considerable unity, however, about what they disliked:

✓ "a sense of invisibility"

✓ "a sense of not belonging to the center"

✓ "low respect"

✓ "lack of recognition"

✓ "feeling unwelcome"

✓ "asked to clean too much"

✓ "excluded from chats as well as professional discussions"

✓ and of course: "low pay."

There are fairly simple remedies for many of these common complaints. Make sure you greet a substitute with a friendly welcome. Introduce her or him to the staff and the children. Perhaps everyone can wear name tags or do a name game or song, or you can have a "picture board" on the wall with all the children's names and photos. All this may sound obvious, but it's startling to hear how often these basic gestures are not made. Taking substitutes for granted or sending them to work without a greeting sets a negative tone which may never be overcome. The substitute may already be mentally crossing your program off her list.

Develop a brief handout on each classroom for substitutes and give them a few minutes to look it over. Preferably, each substitute should also have a "buddy" to whom she can go throughout the day with any questions. Your handout should include:

➠ the daily schedule

➠ basic goals, and any observances or practices unique to the program

➠ the legally required adult-child ratio for this classroom and age group

➠ emergency procedures

➠ where to find first aid equipment, emergency forms, toys and other supplies

➠ a list of all the children in the classroom, with notes on any children who have special needs or who may need particular attention

> **Give substitute caregivers the care they need: it can make your own job less stressful in the long run.**

➠ important rules about safety and the use of equipment

➠ an appropriate description of a substitute's responsibilities: i.e., substitutes should never be left alone to supervise children, or expected to plan the program or conduct parent conferences. (Long-term substitutes, however, might be consulted for their feedback on the curriculum, individual children, etc.)

➠ information about pay policies and ongoing job prospects, such as the rate of pay (including a range based on qualifications); policies about payment for fingerprint clearance, physical exams, TB testing or CPR training if these are required for employment; payment policy about breaks, including lunch; and payroll taxes. (Some centers reimburse substitutes for pre-employment expenses after they have worked for a certain period of time.) Be sure to include information about specific job openings or how the substitute can find out about opportunities at the center; many people choose to substitute as a way to check out whether they would want to work in your program.

You may also want to suggest a few simple "sure success" activities, and give some examples of the kind of guidance and discipline you use with the children. Revise the handout periodically so that substitutes aren't given outdated instructions. The more orientation you provide, the better the substitute's chance of handling things smoothly and efficiently. This minimizes change in the children's routine, and lets substitutes know that their time, energy and talents are valued. And tell substitutes when they can take a break—they shouldn't have to ask!

Introduce substitutes to parents at the beginning or end of the day. Be sure to inform parents about your substitute policies and the kinds of orientation or training that substitutes receive. Parents will appreciate this, because it can be unsettling to see unfamiliar faces among the staff. One center, for example, uses a simple one-page form, filled out by the substitute, which is then placed with a Polaroid snapshot on the wall where parents sign in:

> "Please welcome _____,
> who is working today for
> _____ who we expect to
> return on _____. Here
> are some things _____
> would like you to know about
> herself/himself."

The form then includes space for a few lines, such as, "I have two children ages 3 and 6, I have subbed frequently in 10 local centers, and my favorite activity with children is music."

When the day is through—and if you want substitutes to return—thank them and let them know you enjoyed working together. And pay substitutes promptly! It's also a nice gesture for someone on the staff to make a follow-up phone call to substitutes to discuss how the day went, offer some constructive feedback, and ask which things could be changed or improved.

As much as possible, include substitutes in staff discussions; a frequent substitute might be invited to attend staff meetings or in-service training. Invite substitutes to events and parties at the center, too. These gestures foster a sense of belonging and make substitutes feel appreciated, encouraging them to stay on your substitute list.

I I I

Evaluate your substitute policy periodically. Talk about activities or instructions that are particularly easy or hard for temporary staff to handle. Certain regular routines may have to be adjusted if they prove too demanding for a novice. Identify substitutes you think are qualified to become permanent teachers and develop a plan to recruit them to your program. Make time for the permanent staff to talk about the challenging process of continually orienting new people and adjusting to new faces and different teaching styles.

If you take the time to give substitute caregivers the care they need, it can make your work less stressful in the long run. But remember that there is an industry-wide shortage of trained teaching personnel for child care, requiring strategies that go well beyond individual center policies. For a discussion of community-wide responses to the substitute shortage, see Part 4, page 154.

SECTION 5. PUTTING TOGETHER YOUR TURNOVER REDUCTION PLAN

At the end of Part 2, we discussed how to make a turnover management plan for your program, implementing policies and practices that can help relieve the stress and disruption of turnover whenever it happens. But now that you have examined the aspects of your program that could have a major bearing on causing staff turnover—the work environment, your recruitment and hiring practices, your compensation package, and your substitute system—it's time to put the pieces together into a coherent turnover reduction plan, so that staff departures happen less often. Such a plan, in fact, should be an ongoing part of any child care program's work—something that you periodically revisit, revise and keep up-to-date.

The central idea of a turnover reduction plan is for all of us to move beyond complaining about turnover, and to define meaningful, achievable ways to do something about it, both now and for the future. If all of the goals appear too big, it can be easy to give up—and yet, without a longer-term vision, taking small steps may not seem worthwhile. A turnover reduction plan should include short-term goals and steps for reaching them, as well as

> **The idea is to move beyond complaining about turnover, and to define meaningful, achievable ways to do something about it.**

benchmarks to measure progress toward achieving a high-quality child care workplace.

The process of putting together a plan is very much like the process we discussed for using the Model Work Standards (page 90):

➡ Assess your current policies and practices. If you have been using the chapters of this workbook in order, most of this process is already complete.

➡ Discuss higher and lower priorities for improvement.

➡ Determine the cost for each of your top priorities.

➡ Make an action plan.

➡ Document your progress.

➡ Celebrate and broadcast your accomplishments!

The activity on pages 139-140 is based on the class assignment that many child care programs have completed as part of a "Taking On Turnover" training. Following the activity is a sampling of the variety of turnover reduction plans that programs have implemented.

ACTIVITY

YOUR TURNOVER REDUCTION PLAN

1. Each staff member should answer the following question:

✓ What are the main changes that you believe would make your program a place where staff would stay and be motivated to pursue their professional development? Name at least two changes, but no more than five, and why you think they would improve your program.

2. Staff should then discuss and compare the changes they have suggested. Depending on the size of your program, this could be a simple or complex process. Some centers have devoted staff meetings to the subject, while others have used a survey form or suggestion box, and then tabulated and ranked the results to make a plan. Whichever method you choose, make an effort to discuss these issues with all of your co-workers.

While differences and disagreements will probably emerge, you may also find—as we have consistently found in our turnover training sessions—that directors and teaching staff express very similar desires about how they would like to improve their programs to reduce turnover (see page 73).

✓ What are some of the changes that your co-workers have identified as priorities? Discuss similarities and differences among the lists.

✓ If there are major differences among the lists, what do you believe accounts for these differences?

✓ Based on your conversations with others, how would you adapt your own proposal for reducing turnover at your program?

3. A staff member or a representative committee should be delegated to draft a turnover reduction plan for the program which reflects input from all staff. The plan should include:

✓ the priority areas for action;

✓ estimated costs for each part of the plan;

✓ who will be responsible for implementing each part of the plan;

✓ a timeline; and

✓ steps for evaluating your progress and revising the plan as needed.

4. The staff as a whole should then discuss and finalize the plan.

5. If you have found, after this process, that your program is not able to get a plan off the ground, what were the barriers? What are the primary issues in the organization, and for you personally, that stand in the way of progress? If a lack of openness in communication is the main problem, for example, that may need to be the starting point for trying again soon.

REDUCING TURNOVER: PROFILES OF FIVE CHILD CARE PROGRAMS

How programs approach this planning process, and how quickly they are able to move forward, depends on their size, their decision-making structures, and their levels of trust and openness in communication. While issues of compensation have come up in all the programs we have worked with, these have by no means been the only issues, or necessarily the most pressing ones. Staff communication, staff space, and acknowledgment for work well done were among the many other issues that programs saw as critical. The following are some changes that programs have instituted:

➡ Many have created salary schedules for the first time.

➡ Many have also clarified staff job descriptions, with involvement from all staff.

➡ At one center, staff voted to change from a nine-hour work day (with an unpaid hour off for lunch) to an eight-hour day including a half-hour paid lunch break.

➡ At another center, staff are now able, at their own request, to make their own purchases of equipment and supplies, instead of having the director do this for them.

➡ Site directors at a multi-site agency developed site budgets and were able to gain more control of their own sites' finances.

➡ To improve teaching staff involvement in decision-making, one center created a staff representative position on the Board of Directors, and now requests that a Board member attend staff meetings.

Below, in more detail, are some ways in which five diverse programs have aimed to improve their policies and practices to reduce turnover. These profiles mainly reflect the *first* steps that the programs took as the beginning of a longer process. Most importantly— in every case but one—the staff of these programs now feel motivated and encouraged to take further steps against turnover, because they have seen results and experienced success within a very short time.

Program One

This private nonprofit center with ten teaching staff found the turnover plan relatively easy to initiate because of its small size, and because a high percentage of staff had attended a Taking On Turnover training together. The director identified three priorities: more money to help staff with continuing education, a better substitute list, and more in-service training. The teaching staff priorities were a better substitute list and an annual raise.

At a meeting, the staff agreed that the substitute list was the number-one priority; they felt they had been relying too much on whomever they could get, and because of the difficulty of finding qualified, reliable substitutes, some staff had not been using all of their vacation time. All agreed to work on nurturing stronger relationships with a more consistent group of substitutes.

Next, the staff made a request to the Board for a pay increase, and received a raise of $0.25 per hour for staff who complete three units of continuing education. Because the staff were clear about their needs and priorities, they felt that the Board was more responsive than in the past: without being asked, the Board agreed to a four-percent cost-of-living increase for all staff, their first in two years.

Program Two

In this center, which is similar to Program One, working relationships have not been as clear, and therefore these became the focus of the turnover reduction plan. The director identified an assistant director, a staff lounge, and staff pay raises as the top needs. The staff's top concerns were better team-work, a pay raise, a staff room, an assistant director, and better advance-ment opportunities within the agency.

The program began by calling in an organizational consultant to focus on communication. By working with this consultant, the staff:

➤ agreed to hold bimonthly staff meetings;

➤ clarified the duties around clean-up of the center, which had become a major source of tension;

➤ agreed to hire an assis-tant director, defining her duties to include serving as a mentor for substitutes, and creating a buddy system for each sub to work with a staff member;

➤ decided to use a caterer for lunches, which also freed up some lunch-preparation space for setting up a staff room; and

➤ agreed to focus next on pay issues and opportunities for advancement.

Program Three

At this small, for-profit center, the director held a series of meetings on turnover issues, but most of the teach-ers did not feel listened to. Teaching staff reported that except for incentives

> **Small first steps against turnover can make a staff feel motivated to take further steps, because they have seen results and experienced success.**

to pursue further training, the director dismissed their suggestions as unrealis-tic or inappropriate. As priorities, the teachers had identified respect, open communication, training incentives, and fair and equal pay. In the process of discussing their "wish lists" with each other, they had discovered some discrepancies: while one long-time employee was paid $9.75 per hour, for example, a new teacher with the same qualifications had been hired recently at the rate of $12.00 per hour.

"More than anything," reported one teacher, "we all wished to be treated with a funda-mental degree of respect. That means being highly involved in any dialogue that relates to changes in policy affecting the chil-dren and our work." An example she cited was the expectation from the direc-tor and the owners that teachers would help "sell the program" to prospective parents by holding circle time with children in a certain pre-scribed way, which felt to them more like an artificial performance than an authentic activity. Unfortunately, a turnover reduction plan did not materi-alize after this process, and several teachers left the center.

Program Four

This large corporate-sponsored for-profit center conducted an anonymous survey of all staff (over 70 people) and then tallied the results.

The administrators then held a staff meeting on the subject, and set up a joint administrative/teaching staff committee to summarize the recommendations, which were sent on to corporate headquarters. The corporate sponsors were also asked to visit and learn about staff concerns firsthand. A major issue was the amount of paperwork required for teaching staff, some of whom received paid time to complete it, while others did not. The corporate office has now streamlined the forms which staff use, and gives all staff paid time for the task. But at this time, another widely-mentioned complaint—the presence of only one adult bathroom for over 70 employees—has not been resolved.

Program Five

This large, unionized nonprofit center also conducted a survey of teaching staff, but found that it had to circulate the survey form twice before getting good feedback. The center set up a joint administration/teaching staff committee to study the survey results and make plans, and teaching staff received paid release time for working on it.

A major issue was the center's substitute policies, with substitutes often being sent into classrooms with no orientation. The program set up a formal orientation and job training system for subs. Teaching staff also said that they wanted recognition from each other for work well done; better communication with the administration, which they considered "too distant"; compensatory time for advocacy and professional development activities; and more funds for professional development. These were sorted into issues which could be addressed now and which should be part of the next union contract negotiations. For their next contract, instead of a pay increase, staff are proposing that extra funds be directed toward increasing the number of staff—for instance, by adding a "floater" position.

■ ■ ■

While "taking on turnover" must begin with ourselves and our own child care programs, all of us sooner or later come up against the limits of what we are able to achieve alone. In the final chapter, we turn our attention to ways of reaching out to other programs and other stakeholders in the wider community in order to take unified action.

Part 4

BEYOND INDIVIDUAL PROGRAMS: COMMUNITY EFFORTS TO TAKE ON TURNOVER

Quick: What group of people would do the fastest job of bringing the economy to a halt if they didn't show up for work tomorrow morning?

No, it's not the CEOs of all the multinational corporations. It's not even the President and Congress.

It's you and your colleagues who hold this country together on a daily basis. It's three million or more under-recognized child care teachers and providers, working in centers and homes, who allow other families to seek a livelihood—and often don't earn a decent one themselves, even though they're helping to shape the lives of the next generation at the very tenderest age.

What would the country do without you and your co-workers? As more and more policy makers take a hard look at the American child care system, and develop legislation and funding plans to make it work better, it's time to take this question very seriously. No doubt you have recently seen more than one trusted teacher come and go. You know how difficult it is to recruit skilled people to work in your program, and how deeply children experience a sense of loss. You also know that the answer to this child care crisis isn't simply for parents to pay more; many of them are already stretching to make ends meet.

In the preceding chapters, we focused on ways to tackle turnover within your own child care program.

By now, you may have identified steps you can take to manage turnover better when it happens, or ways to use existing resources to improve your work environment. But these internal changes, essential as they are for reducing turnover and stabilizing the workforce, are insufficient. Truly taking on turnover in child care will require understanding its root causes, and engaging in joint efforts to address them with others beyond your own program.

Tackling turnover is a community-wide effort: Centers can work together to share resources. Directors, teachers and family child care providers can join with parents, trainers, resource and referral agencies and others to advocate for affordable, high-quality child care services, and fair and decent employment for those who provide them. Reducing turnover substantially will mean involving policy makers, and business and labor leaders, at the local, state and national levels. In short, our task is to get *everyone* concerned about our shaky child care system: not only what would happen if we didn't show up for work for one day, but what *will* happen if we allow the child care turnover crisis to continue on its present course.

At this point, you may be bristling at the suggestion of yet another task for your to-do list. Whether you are an administrator or a teacher, you are no doubt working hard every day. Perhaps you even hold a second job. Your family and friends may be impatient because so much of your energy already goes toward your work. You may even be thinking of leaving your job or the child care field yourself. We recognize all of these obstacles. But we also know from experience, and from talking with many teachers and directors over the years, that taking on these issues with others outside your workplace can provide the support and energy you need to face the challenges confronting you daily.

This is not to say that community work is always successful or stress-free. People in the child care field often disagree with each other about solutions, or take out their frustrations on one another. Parents and community leaders, at least initially, may be more concerned about affordable services than turnover or related issues. Often our efforts do not succeed, at least the first time around. Still, working with other stakeholders and programs, it becomes easier to see that:

➡ turnover and the related problems of recruitment affect the whole community, not just your program;

➡ other programs, like yours, are operating with insufficient resources;

➡ economic trends and policy decisions at the local, state and national levels are contributing to recruitment and retention problems;

➡ unlike other educational and social services, the child care field lacks an infrastructure for addressing recruitment and retention issues, including substitutes;

➡ many of the current training and professional development efforts in our field fall short of retaining a skilled workforce, because they don't link training with better compensation.

Working with other programs and members of their community, teachers and directors can also gain:

➡ support from others who face the same challenges, reducing their feelings of isolation and frustration;

➡ suggestions and ideas to try in their programs;

➡ recognition from others of the importance of child care work;

➡ opportunities to assume new leadership roles; and

➡ hope in the possibility of broad-based change in our child care system.

When we feel isolated and frustrated, it's also good to remember how far

> **Our task is to get everyone concerned about what will happen if we allow child care turnover to continue on its present course.**

ADVOCACY AS PROFESSIONAL DEVELOPMENT

How can overburdened teachers and administrators find time to get involved in community efforts to take on turnover? As long as we view advocacy and community work as "extras," rather than as an integral component of our jobs, we will be hard pressed to do so. But professionals in our field must be not only competent practitioners but agents of change. If our profession's goal is to ensure the well-being of young children, then surely it is unprofessional to allow the status quo, which is harmful to children, to go unchallenged.

Ruby Takanishi (1980) calls for developing a workforce comprised of "articulate practitioners," who can speak out about the inadequacies of current services for children—many of which stem from poor working conditions and high turnover among child care workers. To accomplish this rests largely on how child care practitioners are trained to see their roles, and the types of ongoing professional development in which they participate (Whitebook, 1994, 1997). Your program can play a role in creating and supporting a corps of "articulate practitioners" by:

➡ Expanding your definition of professional development activities to include staff participation in community efforts to take on turnover, or related activities to improve child care services.

➡ Encouraging staff to use paid time for professional development to participate in community-wide advocacy and organizing efforts. Professional development does not occur solely in classes and at conferences!

➡ Offering "advocacy leave" as an additional benefit—even if only one or two days per year—so that staff can take paid time to participate in community efforts to improve child care. If your budget doesn't allow such a benefit at this time, decide as a group on the community meetings where you want your center to be represented, and brainstorm how to make it possible for a staff member to attend. (Remember, in selecting this person, that it doesn't have to be someone in an administrative role. Community meetings are often a great opportunity for teaching staff to develop as leaders—and teachers contribute a much-needed voice to the discussion of problems and solutions.)

➡ Dedicating a portion of each staff and parent meeting to providing information about events and efforts to improve child care. Allow people time during meetings, for example, to write letters to a policy maker.

➡ Joining your local Worthy Wage Campaign or other groups focused on improving child care, and making sure that all staff receive information about child care events and policy developments at the local and national levels. ★

we have come. When the Center for the Child Care Workforce began in 1978 as the Child Care Employee Project, we seemed to know personally every single advocate in the country working to improve child care jobs, because our numbers were so few. Now, the people advocating for worthy wages and decent child care working conditions are far too numerous to count, and although we still have a long way to go, the issues facing the child care workforce have finally gained much greater media attention, and have become much more prominent on the nation's policy agenda.

WHY WE NEED COMMUNITY-WIDE EFFORTS TO TAKE ON TURNOVER

Even if you follow every suggestion in the preceding chapters, your program may still face a level of turnover that undermines your ability to provide good care. If you've done a calculation of turnover costs in your program, you've probably documented that the problem is gobbling huge amounts of time and money in your program, both of which are scarce. The high levels of turnover in our field reflect two major, interrelated child care problems:

➡ insufficient and often misdirected resources for child care;

> If our profession's goal is to ensure the well-being of young children, then surely it is unprofessional to allow the status quo, which is harmful to children, to go unchallenged.

➡ a lack of infrastructure, which forces individual programs to try to handle system-wide problems on their own, such as securing substitutes or replacement staff.

Insufficient and misdirected resources

Compared to other industrialized countries, the United States invests relatively little in services for young children before they enter school, or to care for older children after school hours. The funding steams supporting services for young children are numerous and complex, yet by any estimation they fail to add up to a coherent, smoothly running system (Cohen, 1996).

Instead, services are often unavailable or unaffordable, or both, for families who need them; researchers repeatedly rate most U.S. child care as poor or mediocre in quality (Whitebook, Howes & Phillips, 1990; Helburn, 1995; Kontos et al., 1995); and the child care workforce is so poorly paid that it is very difficult to recruit and retain skilled staff. High-quality care is more costly to provide than what most parents can afford to pay. As a result, the child care system inevitably needs another source of funds to break the unfair link between what parents pay for care—often too much—and what child care workers earn—almost always too little (Bellm, 1994).

More resources, however, are only part of the challenge. How the resources are directed determines whether they will lead to better child care jobs and services, or will only expand the existing supply of mediocre services and undesirable jobs. Unfortunately, there has been a strong policy trend in recent years toward expanding the quantity of available child care, with relatively very little focus on investing in quality.

Over the past decade, we have witnessed an enormous increase in public dollars for child care. More child care centers received public dollars in 1997 than in 1988, which has allowed more of them to assist low-income families with child care costs. But because this increased public funding for child care was rarely targeted to quality improvements or increased compensation, these dollars have not resulted in better wages or lower staff turnover. In fact, the sector of the industry characterized by the lowest wages—the for-profit chains—has experienced the greatest increase in access to public subsidies. Meanwhile, real wages for most child care teaching staff have remained stagnant since the late 1980s (Whitebook, Howes & Phillips, 1998).

There has also been considerable support for financing the child care system through increased tax credits for parents and employers—but this method, while it can somewhat ease parents' and employers' financial burdens, does very little to address child care quality and staffing issues, because there are no guarantees or guidelines for how these revenues will be spent.

A lack of infrastructure

Consider the following scenarios:

SCENARIO ONE: Teacher A wakes up one morning with a fever and a sore throat. She knows she should stay home for her own well-being and the sake of the children, but she is disappointed about missing the exciting lesson she planned for the day. She places a single phone call to say she won't be coming in. Then she returns to bed and promptly falls back to sleep, assured that a qualified teacher will take over her classroom.

SCENARIO TWO: Teacher B also wakes up with a fever and sore throat, but she faces a different set of emotions and choices. If she stays home, she will not just miss the field trip she'd been looking forward to; she knows the trip will probably be canceled if she can't find a substitute, and the children will be upset. Even if she wants to stay home, she probably can't locate a substitute on such short notice, or at least one who won't ruin her co-teacher's day. She feels angry just thinking about having to call for a substitute, but the policy is that everyone arranges coverage for themselves except in an emergency. So is this an emergency? She tries to tell herself she doesn't feel that bad, and gets up to get ready for work. It doesn't seem worth the trouble to stay home and take care of herself. But it's another reason why she thinks about quitting her job.

As you've probably guessed, Teacher A works in a public elementary school and Teacher B works in a child care center. Public schools have a system in place for securing substitutes or replacement staff. Usually the district office, which coordinates the needs of many schools in a community, deals with all issues of recruitment and classroom coverage. These systems may not work perfectly, but they function sufficiently well so that teachers are able to stay home when sick. Schools, in addition, usually have a system in place for buying supplies in bulk, and for recruiting new staff, working in close cooperation with local colleges and universities.

With few exceptions, child care centers have none of these types of support. Each separate organization is trying to find replacements and figure out how to attract staff. Many directors and teachers spend a part of their evenings or weekends shopping for supplies and food. The local resource and referral agency may mail a monthly substitute list to centers, but the substitutes probably haven't been interviewed or screened, the most skilled people on the list are quickly offered permanent jobs, and those who remain are often unsuited to child care work. The absence of a support structure for basic industry services leads to highly inefficient duplications of effort, and it greatly increases the sense of frustration and burnout so prevalent in the field.

OVERCOMING BARRIERS TO WORKING TOGETHER FOR CHANGE

Even if you feel ready to join with others in the community to bring about changes in our child care system, you may feel at a loss about how to go about it. In the course of working on these issues over the years, we have identified three common barriers that keep people from working together for change:

➡ narrow definitions of who is responsible for solving problems related to child care staffing and quality;

➡ a lack of awareness of potential solutions; and

➡ the isolation that many programs and practitioners suffer.

Below, we explore each of these barriers and suggest some strategies to overcome them.

Narrow definitions of who is responsible for improving child care staffing and quality

Child care staffing issues affect a great number of people beyond those who use or provide these services. Yet there is a general attitude in the U.S. that any job-related dissatisfaction is merely a personal issue: if you think you are undervalued or underpaid, you should do what it takes to "get a better job;" if your child care business is struggling, it must mean you aren't managing it right. These attitudes are related to the pervasive belief that arrangements for young children are problems for individual families to solve, rather than society as a whole. Even though child care is a social good that potentially benefits everyone, a limited view of who is responsible for improving it restricts the flow of resources to child care programs.

By contrast, most Europeans believe that child care costs should not exceed 10 percent of family incomes and that public subsidies should cover 70-80 percent of those costs. As a consequence, in many European countries, families have universal access to early education and care, while in the U.S., public subsidies cover less than half the cost of care, and subsidies are generally tied to welfare status and poverty levels, but are grossly inadequate to meet the needs of most eligible families. The U.S. approach also results in a two-tiered system: limited subsidies for the poor, and child and dependent care tax credits for eligible middle-class families (Foundation for Child Development, 1998).

ACTIVITY

CHILD CARE STAFFING AND TURNOVER: WHOSE PROBLEM IS IT?

At a staff or community meeting:

➡ Brainstorm a list of all the categories of potential stakeholders for quality child care in your community: for example, parents, employers, elementary school teachers and principals, representatives of youth organizations, unions and union members, and city council members or other elected officials. How does turnover affect people in each group?

➡ Next, if possible, identify specific individuals in each group.

➡ List what you think keeps these stakeholders from getting involved, such as lack of information about the problem. (If you aren't sure, you might interview a couple of people in each category to find out).

➡ Identify what resources and power these different stakeholders could bring to the table.

➡ Brainstorm what each group may need in order to be swayed, and ways to involve them in your efforts. You may not be able to involve all the stakeholders soon or easily, but having a picture of potential allies (or opponents) is important as you develop a community strategy to take on turnover. Remember to share with them your calculations of the costs of turnover in your program—both in dollars and in lost opportunities (pages 65-68). This information can be very startling and persuasive!

Working for change is an overwhelming prospect if you think that you and your co-workers are the only ones available to help. But increasingly, U.S. policy makers and business and labor leaders are beginning to see child care as something they have a stake in, and are getting involved in crafting solutions, with encouragement and input from child care practitioners like you.

Lack of awareness of potential solutions

Learning about how others have taken on turnover can "jump start" your thinking about what you might do in your own community. During the past decade, a significant number of efforts to improve child care jobs have been implemented or explored at the federal and local levels. The federally-funded Head Start program, and U.S. Army Child Development Services, have devoted major portions of their funding since 1990 to improving staff salaries.

Also begun in 1990, the Child Care and Development Block Grant has permitted states to use federal child care quality improvement funds specifically for staff compensation initiatives. While only a very modest portion of states' child care funds have gone for this purpose, their availability gave rise to a number of promising programs linking

---

ACTIVITY

HOW HAVE PEOPLE MADE A DIFFERENCE IN SOLVING CHILD CARE STAFFING AND TURNOVER PROBLEMS?

At a staff or community meeting:

➠ Discuss the various ways in which child care jobs could be improved; for example, better health or retirement benefits, salary enhancements, financial assistance with education and training, mentoring, unionizing, etc. It is also useful to explore how other groups of workers, such as nurses, public school teachers or secretaries, have joined together to address similar problems, or how child care is funded and organized in other countries.

➠ Prioritize your interest in various strategies.

➠ Assign people to research each of the areas, and schedule time at upcoming meetings for people to report on different topics. (If at all possible, staff members should be able to do their research on paid time; this is a professional development activity, too!) In a short period, everyone on staff or in your community group will be better informed and better able to analyze appropriate strategies for your area.

ACTIVITY

HOW CAN YOU CONNECT YOUR
CHILD CARE PROGRAM WITH OTHERS?

➡ Think about two things you can do to bring yourself into contact with others outside your program. You don't necessarily have to join an ongoing group. You might begin by attending a workshop or one-day conference, or calling someone at another center and making a date to visit.

➡ If you already feel connected with other child care programs, reach out to someone who isn't, and invite this person to join you in a community activity or to visit your program.

---

training with better compensation, often through mentoring, loan or grant programs. Better health and retirement benefits for child care workers are also being explored in some states, as well as efforts to improve work environments through the use of CCW's Model Work Standards and through collective bargaining (with union drives taking place in several states).

These various initiatives are highlighted in several publications available from the Center for the Child Care Workforce:

✓ *Breaking the Link*: A National Forum on Child Care Compensation (1994)

✓ *Salary Improvements for Head Start*: Lessons for the Early Care and Education Field (1995)

✓ *Early Childhood Mentoring Programs*: A Survey of Community Initiatives (1996)

✓ *Making Work Pay in the Child Care Industry*: Promising Practices for Improving Compensation (1997)

✓ *Creating Better Child Care Jobs*: Model Work Standards for Teaching Staff in Center-Based Child Care (1998)

✓ our biannual news and information bulletin, *Rights, Raises, Respect*.

Isolation of programs and practitioners

In some communities, child care center directors and teachers rarely talk with their counterparts in other programs. This keeps us from benefiting from each other's expertise, sharing ideas about how to address problems, or coming up with collective solutions to share the burden. At one of our turnover training sessions, for example, several directors who seldom went to meetings were surprised to learn about a source of substitutes connected to a senior community center, while other centers had been relying upon it regularly. Similarly, a teacher was surprised to learn that her counterparts in other centers were paid extra when parents picked up their children late; she had routinely worked beyond her scheduled hours without additional pay, even though the center charged a late fee to parents. By learning about other options, she realized she had the right to better treatment, and was able to ask successfully for a change in her center's policy.

Joining together can help programs ensure that resources are targeted in ways that will really help. In a number of communities, for example, businesses have provided some support for centers seeking NAEYC accreditation. In a recent study of centers in three communities, we found that those which had previously worked together as a group, and had helped define the type of support they needed, were more successful in achieving accreditation (Whitebook, Sakai & Howes, 1997).

MAKING A TURNOVER ACTION PLAN AT THE COMMUNITY LEVEL

At the end of Part 3, we outlined the steps involved in making a turnover reduction plan for your program, and the same steps apply to undertaking a project at the community level—even if you begin small, with only one or two other people:

- develop a plan

- assess what you want to accomplish as a group

- set some goals

- delegate tasks

- implement your decisions,

- evaluate and celebrate your progress, and

- identify your next set of goals or objectives.

You will also need to address leadership and diversity issues. This may be as simple as deciding to rotate chairing responsibilities to ensure that everyone is participating fully. But it may also involve taking stock of who isn't represented in your group, whom to invite if your group expands, and what types of activities you can reasonably undertake, given your composition. If you decide to plan a community-wide substitute pool, for example, you will need representatives from many programs to help you design a system that works. Ideally, you would also involve people working as substitutes, in order to shape a system that meets their needs. In contrast, if you are considering sharing the services of a translator—an idea that surfaced often in our California turnover training sessions, because many programs serve families from diverse linguistic groups—an effective plan could involve as few as two programs.

The following discussion highlights three types of collective solutions that administrators, teachers and others have undertaken in recent years. The first two, which emerged from our Taking On Turnover trainings, are more modest in scope, because the work groups were limited by the duration of the class. The third, a California coalition to develop and promote a child care compensation bill in the state legislature, reflects a more ongoing relationship and level of commitment among the participants.

For more information and guidance about starting an activist group in your community, see the Center for the Child Care Workforce publication, *Grassroots Organizing: A Handbook for Child Care Teachers and Family Child Care Providers* (CCW, 1997).

Using the Cooperative Business Development Survey

In Part 3, we suggested filling out this survey to assess how your program might save on certain services and invest these savings in staff compensation. If your community has a local directors' or teachers' group, you might bring the survey to a meeting and ask everyone to fill it out. Once you have summarized the responses, you will probably have identified a number of services that child care programs in your area could consider sharing. Many centers, for example, are required to purchase a formal financial audit each year. If a group of centers solicits bids together, auditors may be more than willing to reduce their per-center rate in exchange for guaranteed business from several programs. Child care programs have also identified the bulk purchase of supplies as a possible joint effort.

During one of our turnover trainings, participants from two centers discovered that they had both approached the

same local food service at a nearby hospital about providing meals for their programs. The food service had been unable to accommodate them, because neither center met the minimum requirement for the number of daily meals. Staff from the two centers then returned to the vendor and were able to negotiate a joint contact, with a modest fee for the second drop-off. As a result, each center was able to rearrange staff duties and save several thousand dollars per year. The funds were reinvested in a "floater" staff position at one center, and for increased planning and preparation time for teaching staff at the other. In this case, the survey helped the two programs to break through a barrier they had been unable to overcome on their own.

Seeking Community-Wide Solutions to Substitute Problems

Sooner or later, discussions of turnover lead to the issue of substitutes. During our trainings, we asked participants to engage in two discussions about substitutes. First, after they had completed the assessment of their programs' substitute practices (Part 3, page 129), we asked the group to list barriers to finding and keeping good substitutes that were beyond their individual programs' control.

In several communities, the process and costs involved in securing fingerprints for criminal background checks (required for all child care employees) were a major aggravation. The processing fee for each new substitute was adding up to a substantial monthly expenditure for many centers. In fact, some administrators confessed to waiting to see whether a substitute would work out before submitting the paperwork, and delays in receiving clearance reports meant that substitutes were often long gone before their fingerprints were cleared. Substitutes were frustrated because their fingerprint clearance was often not transferred from one program to the next, and some centers required them to pay for it. Following the training, a few representatives from the group agreed to meet with local licensing representatives and the resource and referral agency, and were able to identify steps to reduce a major source of frustration for many programs.

Next, we asked participants to design an ideal substitute system for their community. At first, people found the task very difficult, talking in terms of what they already had in place and borrowing ideas from each other, but unable to think beyond these current limits. Once they were encouraged to think about what they should really have in an ideal situation, however, the ideas began to flow. The following plan for a workable community-based substitute system—a collaboration between child care programs, resource and referral agencies (R&Rs) and community colleges—was drafted at one of the training sessions.

> Once people got beyond thinking in terms of the substitute system they have now, and focused on what they really want, ideas began to flow.

➡ The system would conduct active, ongoing recruitment through public service announcements and other means, recognizing that new substitutes will always be needed. Substituting could become a significant entry point on the career ladder and a way of bringing new people into the field. One of the partners—perhaps the R&R agency—would conduct the recruitment campaign, targeting such people as retired teachers, who might be interested in such work even if they do not wish to become permanent child care employees. This recruitment function could also be part of a community Career Resource Center that would inform practitioners and the public more broadly about options in early childhood education.

➡ The community or four-year college Early Childhood Education Department would help place students as substitutes in child care programs, and perhaps offer a course on being a substitute. Unlike in K-12 education, the linkage in child care between training institutions and service providers is too often informal or disconnected.

➡ The R&R (or another agency) and participating child care centers would advertise jointly for substitutes, sharing the costs for running an ongoing general ad. The R&R would then conduct an initial screening interview, a regular (perhaps monthly) training and orientation session, and some preliminary matching or placement, perhaps even taking calls and dispatching substitutes. Substitutes would be pre-screened and classified according to the age groups they would like to work with, professional background (training, experience, credentials, etc.), the geographical area they can work in, language skills, hours available, transportation needs, and so on. Substitutes might be asked—though it may not be possible to require or enforce this—to agree to stay in the substitute program for a given length of time, during which they would not take a permanent child care job.

➡ Participating child care center teachers and directors would share the responsibility for conducting the training and orientation of substitutes at the R&R office, and would pay an amount for the substitute system's services in proportion to center size. The training and orientation would cover the nature of the job, workplace rights, ideas for classroom activities, and health and safety and emergency procedures. Running these training sessions could be an excellent leadership and mentoring opportunity for teachers. Ideally, centers would also arrange for a paid site visit by each new substitute before she or he was hired to work.

Following the training, several participants agreed to continue meeting to refine the plan, analyze costs, and arrange for follow-up meetings with funders and policy makers. Several foundations were interested in the idea, and participants also considered approaching state policy makers about using federal child care quality improvement funds to support the effort.

Crafting a Statewide Compensation Initiative

The community efforts described so far could alleviate some of the problems related to turnover, but they do not address improving wages, a key to successful staff recruitment and retention. While we are far from having a fully-funded child care system, it doesn't mean that nothing can be changed until we have all the funds we need. There are increasing numbers of examples of successful, if modest, community efforts to improve wages; the following effort was undertaken by California advocates in 1998.

Responding to increased public discussion of child care, a growing staffing crisis fueled by the upturn in the economy and class size reduction, and frustration about the slow pace of change occurring through state agencies, a coalition of child care advocates—including teachers, family child care providers, directors, trainers, resource and referral staff and others—decided to initiate a legislative proposal to improve salaries. The starting

HIGHLIGHTS OF THE CALIFORNIA C.A.R.E.S. BILL
(COMPENSATION AND RECOGNITION ENHANCES STABILITY)

The C.A.R.E.S. bill would establish a program to build and reward a skilled and stable child care workforce throughout the state. California C.A.R.E.S. would be comprised of two major programs, the "Child Development CORPS" and "Resources for Retention":

➡ The **Child Development CORPS** would include family child care providers and center-based staff (including teachers, site supervisors and directors) who meet certain education and training qualifications, commit to continuing their professional development for at least 21 hours per year, and agree to provide child care services for a specified period of time. Members of the CORPS would receive monetary rewards ranging from $500 to $6,500 per year, depending on their education and background.

➡ **Resources for Retention** would provide additional support to public and private child care programs which are committed to improving quality, by providing differential reimbursement rates and Quality Improvement Rewards to assist programs in achieving accreditation, improving staff retention, and making progress toward meeting state-recommended compensation guidelines (Burton & Whitebook, 1998). ★

point of the discussion was to analyze an existing model used in several states, called T.E.A.C.H., for linking compensation and training. The group then identified the components of a program that would meet the needs of California's child care workforce, many of whom have invested heavily in education and training for child care careers but are leaving for better jobs.

The outlines of a proposal were drafted, and the group then solicited feedback from a wide range of people—including publicly and privately funded programs, family child care programs and centers, administrators and teaching staff—through a series of meetings and mailings. Another round of revision occurred, a legislative author was identified, and a bill named California C.A.R.E.S. was drafted (see the accompanying chart of highlights). Then came the arduous process of shepherding the bill through the legislative process, accomplished by the joint efforts of representatives from several organizations. Many advocates throughout the state also visited their

---

ACTIVITY

TWO STEPS FORWARD

Write down two things you can do to get involved with others who are committed to taking on turnover and upgrading child care jobs. Copy this list, give it to someone else, and ask her to mail it to you in two months. Offer to mail a list for her as well!

ACTIVITY

YOUR VISION OF THE FUTURE

Envision the kind of child care workforce you would like to see in your community in five years. What steps need to be taken in order to get there? What are the barriers to be overcome? Try doing this just for yourself and with your co-workers, or in a local group. The answers will become your priority list.

---

representatives on Worthy Wage Day, May 1, and at other times, to emphasize the bill's importance. In the process, the bill was reduced from $50 million (the initial estimate of what it would take to ensure that all child care workers earned a wage commensurate with their education and training) to $5 million (a sufficient amount to pilot the program in several communities).

Due to an impressive outpouring of public support, the bill passed both houses of the California legislature. Although it was vetoed by the Governor, a disappointing climax to the nearly year-long effort, the child care community knew that it had accomplished far more than it ever thought possible at the onset, and

renewed its commitment to succeeding the following year in getting the program funded.

▮ ▮ ▮

There is no single right way to be involved in community efforts to take on turnover. Some might be small, and some might be on a grand scale. The point is to get started, no matter how small the effort, and yet to think big.

If we only ask for what we think we are likely to get, we limit our own vision severely before we have even begun, and we hold back from taking actions that could succeed after all.

Don't hesitate...get started today!

REFERENCES AND FURTHER READING

Ainsworth, M.D., Blehar, M., Waters, E. & Wall, S. (1978). *Patterns of Attachment: A Psychological Study of the Strange Situation.* Hillsdale, N.J.: Erlbaum.

Anderson, C., Nagel, R., Roberts, W. & Smith, J. (1981). "Attachment to substitute caregivers as a function of center quality and center involvement." *Child Development* 52, 53-61.

Anderson, C.S. (1982). "The search for school climate: A review of the research." *Review of Educational Research* 52(3), 368-420.

Balfour, D.L. & Neff, D.M. (1993). "Predicting and managing turnover in human service agencies: A case study of an organization in crisis." *Public Personnel Management* 22(3), 473-486.

Bellm, D. (1994). *Breaking the Link: A National Forum on Child Care Compensation.* Washington, D.C.: Center for the Child Care Workforce.

Bellm, D., Burton, A., Shukla, R. and Whitebook, M. *Making Work Pay in the Child Care Industry: Promising Practices for Improving Compensation.* (1997). Washington, D.C.: Center for the Child Care Workforce.

Belsky, J. & Cassidy, J. (1994). "Attachment: Theory and evidence." In R. Rutter, D. Hay & F. Baron-Cohen, eds., *Developmental Principles and Clinical Issues in Psychology and Psychiatry,* 323-402. Oxford: Blackwell.

Bittel, L.R. & Newstrom, J. (1990). *What Every Supervisor Should Know.* New York: McGraw-Hill.

Bloom, P.J. (1993). "'But I'm worth more than that!': Implementing a comprehensive compensation system." Washington, D.C.: National Association for the Education of Young Children. *Young Children,* May 1993, 67-72.

Bloom, P.J. (1997). "Decision-making influence: Who has it? Who wants it?" *Child Care Information Exchange,* March 1997, 6-14.

Bloom, P.J. (1997). *A Great Place to Work: Improving Conditions for Staff in Young Children's Programs,* Revised Edition. Washington, D.C.: National Association for the Education of Young Children.

Bloom, P. J. (1996). *Improving the Quality of Work Life in the Early Childhood Setting: Resource Guide and Technical Manual for the Early Childhood Work Environment Survey.* (Rev. ed). Wheeling, Ill.: National-Louis University.

Bloom, P.J. (in press). "Using climate assessment to improve the quality of work life in early childhood programs." *Advances in Early Education and Day Care.*

Bloom, P.J., Sheerer, M. & Britz, B. (1991). *Blueprint for Action: Achieving Center-Based Change Through Staff Development.* Mt. Ranier, Md.: Gryphon House.

Bowlby, J. (1969; second edition, 1982). *Attachment and Loss: Vol. 1. Attachment.* New York: Basic.

Bowlby, J. (1973). *Attachment and Loss: Vol. 2. Separation.* New York: Basic.

Bowlby, J. (1980). *Attachment and Loss: Vol. 3. Loss, Sadness and Depression.* New York: Basic.

Bretherton, I. (1985). "Attachment theory: Retrospect and prospect." *Monographs of the Society for Research in Child Development,* 50 (1-2, Serial No. 209), 3-35.

Bureau of Labor Statistics. (1996). *Occupational Employment Statistics (OES) Program Survey.* Washington, D.C.: U.S. Department of Labor.

Bureau of Labor Statistics. (1998). *Occupational Projections and Training Data.* Washington, D.C.: U.S. Department of Labor.

Burton, A. & Whitebook, M. (1998). *Child Care Staff Compensation Guidelines for California 1998.* Washington, D.C.: Center for the Child Care Workforce.

Burton, A., Whitebook, M., Sakai, L., Babula, M. & Haack, P. (1994). *Valuable Work, Minimal Rewards: A Report on the Wisconsin Child Care Work Force.* Washington, D.C.: Center for the Child Care Workforce, and Madison, Wis.: Wisconsin Early Childhood Association.

Center for the Child Care Workforce. (1998a). *Creating Better Child Care Jobs: Model Work Standards for Teaching Staff in Center-Based Child Care.* Washington, D.C.: Center for the Child Care Workforce.

Center for the Child Care Workforce. (1998b). *Current Data on Child Care Salaries and Benefits in the United States.* Washington, D.C.: Center for the Child Care Workforce.

Center for the Child Care Workforce. (1997). *Grassroots Organizing: A Handbook for Child Care Teachers and Family Child Care Providers.* Washington D.C.: Center for the Child Care Workforce.

Center for the Child Care Workforce, & Worker Options Resource Center. (1997). *Rights in the Workplace: A Guide for Child Care Teachers.* Washington, D.C.: CCW and WORC.

Coelen, C., Glantz, F. & Calore, D. (1979). *Day Care Centers in the U.S.: A National Profile 1976-1977.* Cambridge, MA: Abt Books.

Cohen, A. J. (1996). "A brief history of federal financing for child care in the United States." In Behrman, ed. *The Future of Children,* 26-40. Los Altos, Calif.: Center for the Future of Children, The David and Lucile Packard Foundation.

Creery, P. (1986). "The high cost of turnover." *ABA Banking Journal,* September 1986, 113-114.

Dawson, C. (1988). "Costing labour turnover through simulation proesses: A tool for management." *Personnel Review* 17(4), 29-37.

Derman-Sparks, L. & the ABC Task Force. (1989). *Anti-Bias Curriculum.* Washington, D.C.: National Association for the Education of Young Children.

Erickson, M.F., Sroufe, L.A. & Egeland, B. (1985). "The relationship between quality of attachment and behavior problems in preschool in a high-risk sample." In I. Bretherton & E. Waters, eds., "Growing points of attachment theory and research." *Monographs for the Society for Research in Child Development 50* (1-2, Serial No. 209), 147-166.

Foundation for Child Development. (1998). "FCD Update/March '98." New York: Foundation for Child Development.

Gomby, D. et al. (1996). "Financing child care: Analysis and recommendations." In Behrman, ed. *Financing Child Care*, 5-25. Los Altos, Calif.: Center for the Future of Children, The David and Lucile Packard Foundation.

Gonzalez-Mena, J. (1993). *Multicultural Issues in Child Care*. Mountain View, Calif.: Mayfair.

Goosen, F.A. & van IJzendoorn, M. (1991). "Quality of infant attachments to professional caregivers: Relation to infant-parent attachments and day care characteristics." *Child Development* 61, 832-837.

Greengard, S. (1995). "Leveraging a low-wage work force." *Personnel Journal*, 74(1), 90-102.

Greenman, J. (1996). "So long, it's been not so good to know you." *Child Care Information Exchange*, November 1996, 80-84.

Helburn, S.W., ed. (1995). *Cost, Quality, and Child Outcomes in Child Care Centers. Technical Report*. Denver: University of Colorado at Denver, Department of Economics, Center for Research in Economic and Social Policy.

Howes, C. & Hamilton, C. (1992a). "Children's relationships with caregivers: Mothers and child care teachers." *Child Development* 63, 859-866.

Howes, C. & Hamilton, C. (1992b). "Children's relationships with child care teachers: Stability and concordance with parental attachments." *Child Development* 63, 867-868.

Howes, C. & Hamilton, C. (1993). "The changing experience of child care: Changes in teachers and in teacher-child relationships and children's social competence with peers." *Early Childhood Research Quarterly* 8, 15-32.

Howes, C. & Matheson, C. C. (1992). "Contextual constraints on the concordance of mother-child and teacher-child relationships." *New Directions for Child Development* 57, 26-40.

Howes, C., Phillips, D.A. & Whitebook, M. (1992). "Thresholds of quality: Implications for the social development of children in center-based child care." *Child Development* 63, 449-460.

James, L.R. & Jones, A.P. (1974). "Organizational climate: A review of theory and research." *Psychological Bulletin* 81, 1096-1112.

Johnson, D.W. & Johnson, F.P. (1975). *Joining Together: Group Theory and Group Skills*. Englewood Cliffs, N.J.: Prentice-Hall.

Kim, M. (in press). "Where the grass is greener: Voluntary turnover and wage premiums." *Industrial Relations*. New Brunswick, N.J.: Rutgers University, School of Management and Labor Relations.

Kontos, S. (1992). "The role of continuity and context in children's relationships with nonparental adults." *New Directions for Child Development* 57, 109-119.

Kontos, S., Howes, C., Shinn, M. & Galinsky, E. (1995). *Quality in Family Child Care and Relative Care.* New York: Teachers College Press.

Lynch, M. & Cicchetti, D. (1992). "Maltreated children's reports of relatedness to their teachers." *New Directions for Child Development* 57, 82-107.

Main, M., Kaplan, N. & Cassidy, J. (1985). "Security in infancy, childhood and adulthood: A move to the level of representation." In I. Bretherton & E. Waters, ed., "Growing points of attachment theory and research." *Monographs for the Society for Research in Child Development* 50 (1-2, Serial No. 209), 66-104.

Mercer, M.W. (1998). "Reducing the costs of turnover." *Personnel* 65(12), 36-42.

Mitchell, A., Stoney, L. and Dichter, H. (1997). *Financing Child Care in the United States: An Illustrative Catalog of Current Strategies.* Kansas City, Mo.: The Ewing Marion Kaufman Foundation, and Philadelphia, Pa.: The Pew Charitable Trusts.

Mobley, W.H. (1982). *Employee Turnover: Causes, Consequences and Control.* Menlo Park, Calif.: Addison Wesley.

National Center for Education Statistics. (1994-5). *Integrated Postsecondary Education Data System Finance Survey.* Washington, D.C.: U.S. Department of Education.

National Center for Education Statistics. (1997). *Characteristics of Stayers, Movers and Leavers: Results from the Teacher Follow-up Survey: 1994-95.* Washington, D.C.: U.S. Department of Education.

Parker, D. F., & Rhine, S.L.W. (1991). "Turnover costs and wage-fringe mix." *Applied Economics* 23, 617-622.

Pearce, D. (1996). *The Self-Sufficiency Standard.* Washington, D.C.: Wider Opportunities for Women.

Phillips, D. (1990). "The price tag on turnover." *Personnel Journal*, December 1990, 58-61.

Powell, I., Montgomery, M. & Cosgrove, J. (1994). "Compensation structure and established quit and fire rates." *Industrial Relations* 33(2), 229-248.

Rodd, J. (1994). *Leadership in Early Childhood: The Pathway to Professionalism.* New York: Teachers College Press.

Rousseau, L. (1984). "What are the real costs of employee turnover?" *CA Magazine*, December 1984, 48-53.

Senge, P.M. (1994). *The Fifth Discipline: The Art and Practice of the Learning Organization.* New York: Currency Doubleday.

Steele, F. & Jenks, S. (1997). *The Feel of the Work Place.* Reading, Mass.: Addison Wesley.

Stivison, T. (1992). "Liberal compensation combats turnover." *Credit Union Magazine* 58(4), 42-22.

Tagiuri, R. (1978). *The Concept of Organization Climate*. Ann Arbor, Mich.: University of Michigan, Microfilm International.

Takanishi, R. (1980). "The unknown teacher: Symbolic and structural issues in teacher education." Keynote speech delivered at annual conference of Midwest Association for the Education of Young Children, Milwaukee, Wis.

U.S. Department of Education, National Center for Education Statistics. (1997). *Characteristics of Stayers, Movers and Leavers: Results from the Teacher Follow-Up Survey: 1994-95*. Washington, D.C.: U.S. Department of Education.

van IJzendoorn, M. H., Sagi, A. & Lambermon, M.W.E. (1992). "The multiple caretaker paradox: Data from Holland and Israel." *New Directions for Child Development* 57, 5-24.

Waters, E. & Deane, K.E. (1985). "Defining and assessing individual differences in attachment relationships: Q-methodology and the organization of behavior in infancy and early childhood." In I. Bretherton & E. Waters, eds., "Growing points of attachment theory and research." *Monographs for the Society for Research in Child Development* 50 (1-2, Serial No. 209), 41-65.

White, G.L. (1995). "Employee turnover: The hidden drain on profits." *HR Focus* 72(1), 15-17.

Whitebook, M. (1994). "At the core: Advocacy to challenge the status quo." In Johnson & McCracken, eds. *The Early Childhood Career Lattice: Perspectives on Professional Development*, 68-70. Washington, D.C.: National Association for the Education of Young Children.

Whitebook, M. (1995). *Salary Improvements for Head Start: Lessons for the Early Care and Education Field*. Washington, D.C.: Center for the Child Care Workforce.

Whitebook, M. (1997). "Who's missing at the table?: Leadership opportunities and barriers for teachers and providers." In S.L. Kagan & B.T. Bowman, eds., *Leadership in Early Care and Education*. Washington, D.C.: National Association for the Education of Young Children.

Whitebook, M., Burton, A., Montgomery, D., Hikido, C. & Chambers, J. (1996). *California Child Care and Development Compensation Study: Towards Promising Policy and Practice*. Palo Alto, Calif.: American Institutes for Research, and Washington, D.C.: Center for the Child Care Workforce.

Whitebook, M. & Granger, R.C. (1989). "'Mommy, who's going to be my teacher today?': Assessing teacher turnover." *Young Children*, May 1989. Washington, D.C.: National Association for the Education of Young Children.

Whitebook, M., Howes, C. & Phillips, D. (1990). *Who Cares? Child Care Teachers and the Quality of Care in America*. Final Report of the National Child Care Staffing Study. Washington, D.C.: Center for the Child Care Workforce.

Whitebook, M., Howes, C. & Phillips, D. (1998). *Worthy Work, Unlivable Wages: The National Child Care Staffing Study, 1988-1997*. Washington, D.C.: Center for the Child Care Workforce.

Whitebook, M., Phillips, D. & Howes, C. (1993). *The National Child Care Staffing Study Revisited: Four Years in the Life of Center-Based Child Care*. Washington, D.C.: Center for the Child Care Workforce.

Whitebook, M., Sakai, L. & Howes, C. (1997). *NAEYC Accreditation as a Strategy for Improving Child Care Quality: An Assessment*. Washington, D.C.: Center for the Child Care Workforce.

Willer, B. et al. (1991). *The Demand and Supply of Child Care in 1990: Joint Findings from the National Child Care Survey 1990, and A Profile of Child Care Settings*. Washington, D.C.: National Association for the Education of Young Children.